D1361833

INTRODUCING
ISSUES WITH
OPPOSING
VIEWPOINTS®

Gangs

Mary E. Williams, *Book Editor*

GREENHAVEN PRESS
A part of Gale, Cengage Learning

GALE
CENGAGE Learning·

Detroit • New York • San Francisco • New Haven, Conn • Waterville, Maine • London

Elizabeth Des Chenes, *Director, Publishing Solutions*

© 2012 Greenhaven Press, a part of Gale, Cengage Learning

Gale and Greenhaven Press are registered trademarks used herein under license.

For more information, contact:
Greenhaven Press
27500 Drake Rd.
Farmington Hills, MI 48331-3535
Or you can visit our Internet site at gale.cengage.com

For product information and technology assistance, contact us at

Gale Customer Support, 1-800-877-4253
For permission to use material from this text or product, submit all requests online at www.cengage.com/permissions

Further permissions questions can be e-mailed to permissionrequest@cengage.com

Articles in Greenhaven Press anthologies are often edited for length to meet page requirements. In addition, original titles of these works are changed to clearly present the main thesis and to explicitly indicate the author's opinion. Every effort is made to ensure that Greenhaven Press accurately reflects the original intent of the authors. Every effort has been made to trace the owners of copyrighted material.

Cover image © Binkski/Shutterstock.com.

LIBRARY OF CONGRESS CATALOGING-IN-PUBLICATION DATA

Gangs / Mary E. Williams, book editor.
   p. cm. -- (Introducing issues with opposing viewpoints)
Includes bibliographical references and index.
ISBN 978-0-7377-5679-1 (hbk.)
1. Gangs--Juvenile literature. I. Williams, Mary E., 1960-
HV6437.G343 2012

2011052420

...ted in the United States of America
2 3 4 5 6 7 16 15 14 13 12

Contents

Chapter 3: How Can Gang Violence Be Reduced?

Foreword

I ndulging in a wide spectrum of ideas, beliefs, and perspectives is a critical cornerstone of democracy. After all, it is often debates over differences of opinion, such as whether to legalize abortion, how to treat prisoners, or when to enact the death penalty, that shape our society and drive it forward. Such diversity of thought is frequently regarded as the hallmark of a healthy and civilized culture. As the Reverend Clifford Schutjer of the First Congregational Church in Mansfield, Ohio, declared in a 2001 sermon, "Surrounding oneself with only like-minded people, restricting what we listen to or read only to what we find agreeable is irresponsible. Refusing to entertain doubts once we make up our minds is a subtle but deadly form of arrogance." With this advice in mind, Introducing Issues with Opposing Viewpoints books aim to open readers' minds to the critically divergent views that comprise our world's most important debates.

Introducing Issues with Opposing Viewpoints simplifies for students the enormous and often overwhelming mass of material now available via print and electronic media. Collected in every volume is an array of opinions that captures the essence of a particular controversy or topic. Introducing Issues with Opposing Viewpoints books embody the spirit of nineteenth-century journalist Charles A. Dana's axiom: "Fight for your opinions, but do not believe that they contain the whole truth, or the only truth." Absorbing such contrasting opinions teaches students to analyze the strength of an argument and compare it to its opposition. From this process readers can inform and strengthen their own opinions, or be exposed to new information that will change their minds. Introducing Issues with Opposing Viewpoints is a mosaic of different voices. The authors are statesmen, pundits, academics, journalists, corporations, and ordinary people who have felt compelled to share their experiences and ideas in a public forum. Their words have been collected from newspapers, journals, books, speeches, interviews, and the Internet, the fastest growing body of opinionated material in the world.

Introducing Issues with Opposing Viewpoints shares many of the well-known features of its critically acclaimed parent series, Opposing Viewpoints. The articles are presented in a pro/con format, allowing readers to absorb divergent perspectives side by side. Active reading questions preface each viewpoint, requiring the student to approach the material thoughtfully and carefully. Useful charts, graphs, and cartoons supplement each article. A thorough introduction provides readers with crucial background on an issue. An annotated bibliography points the reader toward articles, books, and websites that contain additional information on the topic. An appendix of organizations to contact contains a wide variety of charities, nonprofit organizations, political groups, and private enterprises that each hold a position on the issue at hand. Finally, a comprehensive index allows readers to locate content quickly and efficiently.

Introducing Issues with Opposing Viewpoints is also significantly different from Opposing Viewpoints. As the series title implies, its presentation will help introduce students to the concept of opposing viewpoints and learn to use this material to aid in critical writing and debate. The series' four-color, accessible format makes the books attractive and inviting to readers of all levels. In addition, each viewpoint has been carefully edited to maximize a reader's understanding of the content. Short but thorough viewpoints capture the essence of an argument. A substantial, thought-provoking essay question placed at the end of each viewpoint asks the student to further investigate the issues raised in the viewpoint, compare and contrast two authors' arguments, or consider how one might go about forming an opinion on the topic at hand. Each viewpoint contains sidebars that include at-a-glance information and handy statistics. A Facts About section located in the back of the book further supplies students with relevant facts and figures.

Following in the tradition of the Opposing Viewpoints series, Greenhaven Press continues to provide readers with invaluable exposure to the controversial issues that shape our world. As John Stuart Mill once wrote: "The only way in which a human being can make some approach to knowing the whole of a subject is by hearing what can be said about it by persons of every variety of opinion and studying all modes in which it can be looked at by every character of mind. No wise man ever acquired his wisdom in any mode but this." It is to this principle that Introducing Issues with Opposing Viewpoints books are dedicated.

Introduction

"Yes, national violent crime rates have dipped . . . but there are areas where [these rates] mean nothing—where children are accustomed to the sounds of gunshots; where young people are lured into gangs; where funerals outnumber weddings."

—Attorney General Eric Holder

I n 2010 the total number of violent crimes in the United States dropped to the lowest rate seen in nearly forty years. The chances of being murdered today are less than half of what they were in the early 1990s, when the national violent crime rate peaked. But in some North American locales, particularly in poor urban and rural communities, violence is on the increase. In Chicago, for example, more than 80 people were shot—and 13 killed—in just two consecutive weekends during the summer of 2010. And near the US border in northern Mexico, more than 23,000 people were murdered between 2006 and 2010. Law enforcement professionals attribute the majority of these shootings and homicides to gangs and other criminal groups.

Gangs have not always been so deadly. In the northeastern United States, the first gangs emerged after the end of the American Revolution, at the turn of the nineteenth century. They were mostly comprised of young males ranging in age from the early teens to the mid-twenties, largely Irish, and eventually also Italian, Jewish, Scandinavian, German, and multiethnic. (In fact, many early gangs were multiethnic, as urban neighborhoods were not strictly segregated at the time). The first gangs of New York were not groups living a life of crime; most members held jobs as common laborers, bouncers, longshoremen, carpenters, butchers, shipbuilders, and the like. With many members also playing important social and civic roles in local immigrant communities, gangs often resembled fraternities or political clubs. While they engaged in violence, "violence was a normal part of their always-contested environment; turf warfare was a condition of the neighborhood,"[1] writes New York historian Luc Sante.

In the late nineteenth and early twentieth century, many gangs merged and branched out, evolving from small neighborhood factions to larger, more organized groups claiming wider territories. Waves of immigrants from Europe and Asia, as well as the migration of Mexicans, Puerto Ricans, and African Americans into large northeastern and Midwestern cities, fueled ethnic and territorial conflicts. Some cities, such as New York, were unprepared for a sudden rise in population and could not provide enough homes for an influx of immigrants. Tenement housing—first seen as a temporary solution—became a long-term reality for most inner-city residents. Dirty, crowded living conditions, poverty, low-wage work, racism, and other social inequities created an environment that fostered conflict and crime. All of these factors helped to establish gangs as part of the social fabric of the urban underclass.

Some gangs specialized in the sale of illegal products and services. Chinese gangs on both the East and West Coasts dominated the opium trade, and leaders of some Italian street gangs were recruited into the Mafia, an organized crime syndicate that made its first large profits selling bootleg alcohol during Prohibition. Other gangs grew because of racial and class conflict and took on a protector role within their communities. The formation of black gangs in Chicago, for example, can be traced to a 1919 riot in which black males confronted white gang members who were terrorizing the African American community. In Los Angeles during the early 1940s, five members of the 38th Street Mexican gang were charged with murder and sentenced to prison after what many believed to be an unfair trial. Their troubles drew the Mexican community into a united struggle against prejudice in law enforcement, and the incarcerated gang members, who maintained a sense of dignity in prison, became folk heroes. Thus, self-defense and resistance against oppression played a role in the development of some early and mid-twentieth-century gangs.

Gang violence increased significantly in the late twentieth century, due in large part to growing profits from illegal drugs—particularly crack cocaine—and the wider availability and variety of firearms. Rather than relying on knives, fists, and occasional handguns, street gang members could now use drug money to buy unprecedented quantities of firearms, including assault rifles and other automatic weapons. Social isolation, police brutality, and poor economic conditions in areas like South Central Los Angeles—with an unemployment rate as high as 50 percent among African American men—resulted in feelings of frustration and resentment in many neighborhoods. This anger provided recruitment opportunities for infamous gangs such as the Bloods and the Crips, who engaged in violent battles over "turf," or drug-selling territory. Drive-by shootings—many of which led to the deaths of innocent bystanders—became standard fare on nightly newscasts. According to the FBI, gang-related homicides in the United States skyrocketed, from 288 in 1985 to a peak of 1,362 in 1993.

In the 2000s the growing phenomenon of gang migration, transnational gangs, and gang recruitment through the Internet has brought new challenges to all regions of the United States. One of today's most dangerous gangs, the Mara Salvatrucha, or MS-13, originated in gang-populated areas of Los Angeles among refugees who had escaped the 1979–1992 Salvadoran civil war. This gang grew in strength as members from Ecuador, Guatemala, Honduras, Nicaragua, and Mexico were allowed to join. In addition, MS-13 members who were arrested in the United States would be deported back to their home countries after being released from prison. They would then join forces with criminal elements in their home country, eventually creating cross-border networks spanning the United States, Mexico, and Central America. Members of MS-13 and other transnational gangs are reportedly hired by international drug cartels to commit robberies and contract killings and to traffic drugs, weapons, and humans. "Operating underneath the big gang players are hundreds of smaller city gangs in neighborhoods all along the border," reports Stratfor Global Intelligence. "These gangs are typically involved in property theft, drug dealing, turf battles, and other forms of street crime that can be handled by local police. However, even these gangs can become involved in cross-border smuggling."[2]

Today's gangs may be more prevalent in urban areas with high concentrations of poverty, but they have spread to suburbs, rural communities, and border regions as well. There is also a growing concern that connections between transnational gangs and smaller gangs in both western and eastern states are strengthening. Many believe that unemployment and economic downturns only increase this gang presence, requiring more effective responses from law enforcement, schools, families, and communities. In *Introducing Issues with Opposing Viewpoints: Gangs* contributors take on several probing questions in the following chapters: "How Serious Is the Problem of Gangs?" "What Causes Gang Violence?" and "How Can Gang Violence Be Reduced?" This exploration provides a thorough overview of one of the most persistent and troubling issues of our time.

Notes

1. Luc Sante. *Low Life: Lures and Snares of Old New York.* New York: Vintage, 1992, p. 198.
2. Quoted in James C. Howell and John P. Moore. "History of Street Gangs in the United States," *National Gang Center Bulletin*, May 2010, p. 17.

Chapter 1

How Serious Is the Problem of Gangs?

A number of social and economic factors have influenced youths to join street gangs.

Gang Membership Is Increasing

Kevin Johnson

"'Most regions in the United States will experience increased gang membership . . . and increased gang-related criminal activity.'"

In the following viewpoint Kevin Johnson discusses the major findings of a report compiled by the US Justice Department's National Gang Intelligence Center. This report concludes that gang membership has significantly increased over the past decade; it also asserts that gangs are responsible for most crimes in communities across the country. A growing number of these gangs are traffickers and distributors of illegal drugs, the author points out. Furthermore, law enforcement officials see a connection between an upsurge in immigrant workers and the growth of gangs in the Midwest and in the South. Gangs are difficult to control because they become savvy to police scrutiny and adapt quickly to changing circumstances, Johnson notes. Johnson is a reporter for *USA Today*, a daily newspaper.

AS YOU READ, CONSIDER THE FOLLOWING QUESTIONS:
  1. According to Johnson, by how much has the gang population in the United States grown since 2005?
  2. How many gang members reside in communities across the United States, according to a report cited by the author? How many gang members live in US prisons or jails?
  3. What is MS-13, according to Johnson?

Criminal gangs in the USA have swelled to an estimated 1 million members responsible for up to 80% of crimes in communities across the nation, according to a gang threat assessment compiled by federal officials.

The major findings in a report by the Justice Department's National Gang Intelligence Center, which has not been publicly released, conclude gangs are the "primary retail-level distributors of most illicit drugs" and several are "capable" of competing with major U.S.-based Mexican drug-trafficking organizations.

"A rising number of U.S.-based gangs are seemingly intent on developing working relationships" with U.S. and foreign drug-trafficking organizations and other criminal groups to "gain direct access to foreign sources of illicit drugs," the report concludes.

The gang population estimate is up 200,000 since 2005.

Bruce Ferrell, chairman of the Midwest Gang Investigators Association, whose group monitors gang activity in 10 states, says the number of gang members may be even higher than the report's estimate.

"We've seen an expansion for the last 10 years," says Ferrell, who has reviewed the report. "Each year, the numbers are moving forward."

A "Growing Threat" Is on the Move

The report says about 900,000 gang members live "within local communities across the country," and about 147,000 are in U.S. prisons or jails.

"Most regions in the United States will experience increased gang membership . . . and increased gang-related criminal activity," the report concludes, citing a recent rise in gangs on the campuses of suburban and rural schools.

Among the report's other findings:

- Last year [2008], 58% of state and local law enforcement agencies reported that criminal gangs were active in their jurisdictions, up from 45% in 2004.
- More gangs use the Internet, including encrypted e-mail, to recruit and to communicate with associates throughout the U.S. and other countries.
- Gangs, including outlaw motorcycle groups, "pose a growing threat" to law enforcement authorities along the U.S.-Canadian border. The U.S. groups are cooperating with Canadian gangs in various criminal enterprises, including drug smuggling.

Assistant FBI Director Kenneth Kaiser, the bureau's criminal division chief, says gangs have largely followed the migration paths of immigrant laborers.

He says the groups are moving to avoid the scrutiny of larger metropolitan police agencies in places such as Los Angeles. "These groups were hit hard in L.A." by law enforcement crackdowns, "but they are learning from it," Kaiser says.

US law enforcement officials meet with officials from El Salvador, Guatemala, Honduras, and Mexico at FBI headquarters. They are discussing the rise of the MS-13 gang and other groups coming into America from Central America.

The MS-13 Gang

One group that continues to spread despite law enforcement efforts is the violent Salvadoran gang known as MS-13.

Michael Sullivan, the departing director of the Bureau of Alcohol, Tobacco, Firearms and Explosives, says the gang's dependence on shocking violence to advance extortion, prostitution and other criminal enterprises has frustrated attempts to infiltrate and disrupt the insular group's activities.

"MS-13's foothold in the U.S. is expanding," Sullivan says.

Kaiser says the street gang is in 42 states, up from 33 in 2005. "Enforcement efforts have been effective to a certain extent, but they (gang members) keep moving," he says.

FAST FACT

Eighty-six percent of cities with a population of at least one hundred thousand report gang activity, according to the US Department of Justice.

MS-13 is the abbreviation for the gang also known as Mara Salvatrucha. The group gained national prominence in the 1980s in Los Angeles, where members were linked to incidents involving unusual brutality.

Since then, it has formed cells or "cliques" across the U.S., says Aaron Escorza, chief of the FBI's MS-13 National Gang Task Force.

The task force was launched in 2004 amid concerns about the gang's rapid spread. Gang members were targeted in broad investigations similar to those used to bust organized crime groups from Russia and Italy.

Law Enforcement Efforts Against MS-13

• *Omaha.* The last of 24 MS-13 members swept up on federal firearms charges and conspiracy to distribute methamphetamine were sentenced last year [2008] in the largest bust since the group emerged there in 2004.

The gang's strength dimmed as a result, but the nine-month probe did not eradicate the group, says Ferrell, who assisted in the investigation.

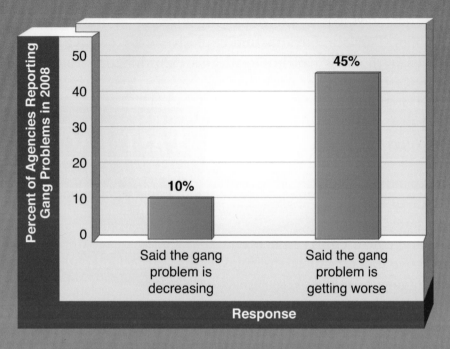

A Worsening Problem

Percent of Agencies Reporting Gang Problems in 2008

10%

45%

Said the gang problem is decreasing

Said the gang problem is getting worse

Response

Taken from: Office of Juvenile Justice Delinquency Prevention, 2009. www.ojjdp.gov.

• *Nashville.* During the past two years [2007–2009], 14 MS-13 members pleaded guilty on charges ranging from murder to obstruction of justice.

Davidson County, Tenn., Sheriff Daron Hall, whose jurisdiction includes Nashville, says MS-13 started growing there about five years ago, corresponding with an influx of immigrant labor.

Last April [2008], county officials began checking the immigration status of all arrestees. "We know we have removed about 100 gang members, including MS-13," to U.S. authorities for deportation, Hall says.

• *Maryland.* This month [January 2009], federal authorities said they had convicted 42 MS-13 members since 2005. More than half were charged in a "racketeering conspiracy" in which members participated in robberies and beatings and arranged the murders of other gang members, according to Justice Department documents.

In one case, Maryland gang members allegedly discussed killing rivals with an MS-13 leader calling on a cellphone from a Salvadoran jail, the documents say.

Escorza says a "revolving door" on the border has kept the gang's numbers steady—about 10,000 in the U.S.—even as many illegal immigrant members are deported.

The FBI, which has two agents in El Salvador to help identify and track members in Central America and the United States, plans to dispatch four more agents to Guatemala and Honduras, Escorza says.

"They evolve and adapt," he says. "They know what law enforcement is doing. Word of mouth spreads quickly."

EVALUATING THE AUTHOR'S ARGUMENTS:

Kevin Johnson maintains that most regions in the United States will experience a rise in gang membership in the coming years. What evidence does he provide to support this assertion? Are you convinced by this evidence?

Gang Attacks on the Public Are Rare

Adam Foxman

"Gang assaults on ordinary citizens who work with police are few and far between."

Authorities would have a better chance of rooting out gang violence if ordinary citizens were more willing to give witness information to police, notes Adam Foxman in the following viewpoint. However, investigations into crimes committed by gangs are often thwarted because the fear of gang reprisal is common. This is due to gang reputation—which instills fear in eyewitnesses and in those who live near gangs—even though violent retaliation against citizens is rare, Foxman points out. A threatening reputation should not prevent people from reporting gang crime anonymously, as the identity of nameless tipsters remains private, the author explains. Foxman is a staff writer for the *Ventura County Star*, a California newspaper.

AS YOU READ, CONSIDER THE FOLLOWING QUESTIONS:

1. According to Mike Matlock, as quoted by the author, what percentage of nongang witnesses are influenced by fear?
2. How do gang members define "respect," according to Foxman?
3. What measures does Crime Stoppers take to protect the identity of anonymous tipsters?

M any involved in the battle against gang crime in Ventura County [California] say ordinary people could do much to break the cycle of violence if they overcame fears of gang retaliation, but authorities concede that's a tall order. Although gang attacks on ordinary citizens who give witness information to law enforcement are rare, fears of such retaliation are widespread, often posing obstacles to gang investigations and prosecutions, authorities and activists say. Oxnard [California] police are now dealing with such fears as they investigate a surge in suspected gang violence this year [2009], the worst the city had seen in years. "It's a big obstacle," Assistant Chief Mike Matlock said. In the two weeks since officers and activists poured into Oxnard's Lemonwood neighborhood after a second killing there in 10 days, violence has dropped. Matlock said detectives are making progress on the 14 serious incidents reported in the first 28 days of the year, but no additional arrests have been made since the initial investigations. The biggest hurdle for detectives is that most of the surviving victims are involved with gangs and have refused to cooperate, Matlock said. Gang members' reluctance to rat each other out, even those from a rival gang, is common around the county, said Senior Deputy District Attorney Derek Malan, one of the county's five gang prosecutors. While they generally play a much smaller role in investigations, Matlock said, authorities have a better chance of making progress with ordinary people reluctant to give information simply because they fear gang retaliation. The problem is difficult to quantify, but investigators estimate roughly half of non-gang witnesses are influenced by fear, Matlock said, yet gang assaults on ordinary citizens who work with police are few and far between. Although it's hard to measure because threats and minor assaults might go unreported, serious assaults always come to police attention because of hospital reporting rules, authorities said.

"It's really a fear that's much greater than reality," Matlock said.

Gang Reputation Based on Fear

Jan Thompson, a Lemonwood resident for almost 37 years, said many of her neighbors are afraid of retaliation from gang members and other bullies, but she doesn't directly know of anyone who has ever been targeted for talking to authorities. She's heard only

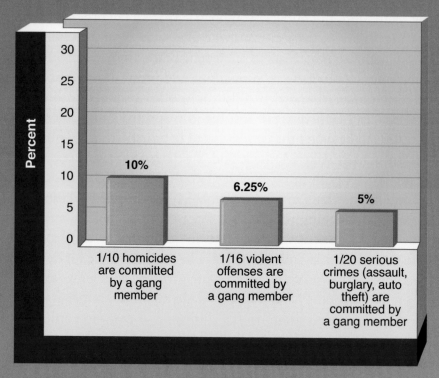

Taken from: Judith Greene and Kevin Pranis. *Gang Wars: The Failure of Enforcement Tactics and the Needs for Effective Public Safety Strategies*, July 2007.

distant rumors of such attacks, she said. Sgt. Bill Schierman, of the Sheriff's Department's west county gang unit, said he doesn't recall any violent gang retaliation against ordinary residents. But gangs don't have to directly attack or threaten people to scare them—they do it by reputation, he said. Fear is a basic element of gang behavior, he said. Gangs build reputations for violence over years, which instills fear. Gang members see it as respect. "Every single gang investigation (has) an element of fear of reprisal," Schierman said. "In some cases, it's harder to get a witness to tell us what happened than to get a confession out of the suspect." In his five years as a gang prosecutor, Malan said, he's handled only two cases involving a witness threatened after cooperating with police, and only one of those involved an injury.

In that case, a boy was beaten unconscious by former gang associates after he testified in juvenile court about a stabbing he witnessed while hanging out with gang members, Malan said. An adult was convicted and sentenced to 18 years in prison in the case. Malan said prosecutors vigorously pursue such cases to protect witnesses, and money is available for witness relocation. But fear can be powerful, he said. "Whether it's real or perceived doesn't really matter as long as there's the perception that there's going to be retaliation. That's what makes our job difficult," Malan said. People must be willing to take a risk to "shine the light of truth" on gang members, he said. "That's how you break the cycle of fear and intimidation—by standing up to them and saying this will not be tolerated, and then letting us step in." For some people in Latino communities, resistance to working with police might be a cultural holdover from countries where authorities could not be trusted, police and activists said. Sandy Montes-Cerna, a board member for the Ventura County chapter of Parents of Murdered Children, said she felt such a reluctance until her nephew, Carlos Prado, 19, was shot to death on March 8, 2006. "It's something that's instilled in you from very young," said Montes-Cerna, who has roots in Costa Rica. Prado's slaying remains unsolved, and Montes-Cerna still hopes someone will come forward with information that could help break open the case. Migrant workers, often targeted by gang members for the cash they frequently carry, are sometimes reluctant to go to police because they might be undocumented. Although Oxnard police work hard to build trust with immigrants and stress to them that officers do not enforce immigration laws, some are still reluctant to make waves, Matlock said. Authorities encourage witnesses worried about retaliation to report crimes anonymously through tip hotlines or Ventura County Crime Stoppers. While they prefer witnesses who can testify in court, law enforcement officials say every bit of information can help.

FAST FACT

According to the Justice Policy Institute, most gang members join when they are young and quickly outgrow their gang affiliation without the help of law enforcement.

Crime Stoppers units across the country do not know the real names of their tipsters. This helps protect the tipsters' identity.

Tipster Identity Is Protected

The Rev. Edgar Mohorko, chairman of the Oxnard Police Clergy Council, said he encourages people to report crime anonymously when he visits neighborhoods hit by gang violence, but many worry that even an anonymous tip can come back to haunt them. Ventura County Crime Stoppers board President Robert Worthley said no one—not even the organization's staff—knows the identities of its tipsters. Whether they call the bilingual hotline center Crime Stoppers contracts with or submit information by text message or through its Web site, tipsters are never asked for their names, Worthley said. Tipsters get only a number they can use to retrieve a reward if the information results in an arrest or indictment. Encryption software conceals texting phone numbers or computer IP addresses, Worthley said, but allows police to send responses asking for more details. "There's absolutely no way their identity is going to be compromised," Worthley said. In January [2009], police made 23 felony arrests as a result of Crime Stoppers tips, and nine of the suspects were alleged gang members, he said.

EVALUATING THE AUTHOR'S ARGUMENTS:

Adam Foxman argues that acts of violent retaliation against regular citizens who witness gang crimes are rare. According to the author of the preceding viewpoint, Kevin Johnson, however, gangs are responsible for up to 80 percent of crimes in communities across the United States. Does Foxman's assertion contradict Johnson's claim that gangs commit a high percentage of crimes? Or do you think that both authors' arguments are valid? Explain your answer.

Growing Numbers of Girls Are Joining Gangs

Sarah Standing

"[It] is becoming a nationwide epidemic: the new breed of British girl gangs."

Young women and girls are joining gangs in increasing numbers, reports Sarah Standing in the following viewpoint. In Great Britain, a rise in crimes committed by girls seems to correspond to the escalation of females in gangs. While poor education, economic recession, and peer pressure are contributing factors, Standing argues that girl gang members are usually the product of dysfunctional or broken families and are acting out of a yearning to belong and be loved. For girls, gang activity often begins as groups of friends wanting to prove themselves by acting tough and edgy, and their behavior eventually escalates into crime. Standing is an associate editor of the *Spectator,* a weekly British magazine.

AS YOU READ, CONSIDER THE FOLLOWING QUESTIONS:

1. What incident involving her daughter alerted the author to the problem of girls in gangs?
2. According to Standing, how many assaults in 2008 were perpetrated by women or female gang members?
3. About how many gangs exist in London, according to the city's Metropolitan Police?

It was a beautiful balmy evening when my youngest daughter finished school last summer. The A-level results had just arrived, and she was happily ambling home from supper with two girl-friends. They were in no rush. They're 18 and were about to spread their wings, leave London for the first time and head off towards various universities. They were finally 'grown up'—with parental curfew lifted, able to judge risks for themselves. And walking along the King's Road in Chelsea [in Greater London], they had little reason to anticipate what was about to befall them.

Three girls approached them, asking the time. They seemed much younger, and their request was innocuous and unthreatening. The street was well lit and, according to my daughter, still buzzing with post-pub stragglers. Suddenly one of the girls turned around and whistled. Only it wasn't an ordinary whistle; it was a call to arms. Within seconds, it was answered. Tilly and her friends were surrounded by a girl-gang who had evidentially been lurking in a side street.

The gang were as professional as they were feral, fast and foul-mouthed. They cunningly separated their victims, yanked a handbag off one friend's shoulder and viciously shoved the other to the ground with brute and unexpected force. They grabbed my daughter's mobile phone out of her hand and, once they had it, scarpered off into the shadows whooping with delight and victory. All random acts of violence are abhorrent, yet there is something about the weaker sex turning on their own that makes the crime seem even more unconscionable.

A New Breed of Girl Gangs

When Tilly and her friends reported the attack to the police, the police wearily took down their details and then made them plough their way through a bulging book of suspects' photos in the futile hope they might be able to identify a face hidden beneath the ubiquitous hoodie. It was, of course, futile. My daughter had fallen victim to something which is becoming a nationwide epidemic: the new breed of British girl gangs.

The figures spell it out. Crimes committed by girls (some as young as ten) have soared by 25 per cent in the last three years. More than half a million assaults last year [2008] were either carried out by women or

Many feel that the state of gangs in Britain today mirrors the gangs depicted in the 1971 movie A Clockwork Orange *(pictured), in which futuristic youth gangs gain respect through acts of violence against pensioners and innocent passer-bys.*

involved female members of gangs. This frightening escalation of girl gang barbarity is apparently rooted in the need to earn 'respect' on the streets. These young thugs seek approbation through violence.

We are living in a terrifying *Clockwork Orange* [a 1962 novel and 1971 film about gangs of the future] environment where aggressively pushing a pensioner or mugging an innocent passer-by gains you kudos and street cred. The media blame all the obvious socio-economic factors such as boredom, binge-drinking, peer pressure, lack of education, truanting, the destruction of the nuclear family, and the absence of father figures, but these girl gang members also appear to have a pathetic underlying yearning to belong. To belong to anything—even a gang—is something to aspire to in the Noughties [slang for the 2000s]. It's a badge of honour.

Why Are Girls Joining Gangs?

For many young women today, proving themselves is apparently no longer about passing exams or getting a decent job. They choose to prove themselves by acting tough. These girls observe the gangster life and actively want to be a part of it. It's perceived as glamorous and edgy, a club they want to join. Gang behaviour starts with petty stuff, just girls hanging out with their friends, then escalates almost imperceptibly. One gang member admitted to a newspaper that 'being part of a gang is a bit like having a big family. You feel safe. You can go anywhere as long as your "bitches" are with you.'

Another girl bragged that belonging to a gang made her feel more confident. 'It's all about having front, attitude and face. I trust my gang more than I do the police. If justice has to be done, I know I can always rely on my gang to follow through.' These cocky 'birds of prey' are no longer mere appendages to male gangs; they're established, autonomous and don't define themselves in relation to men. They routinely carry knives and are prepared to use them.

In London, history is repeating itself; in the early 1970s, the unruly 'bovver birds' rampaged the streets stealing from and assaulting people. But a recent Metropolitan Police estimate put the number of gangs in London at close to 200, of which at least three are known to be exclusively female. Today's girl gangsters have initiation ceremonies—just like the boys—and have to 'prove' themselves by carrying out a street robbery or mugging.

FAST FACT

London police counted thirty gangs of girls—"bovver birds," in the early 1970s. "Bovver" is cockney for "brother," which in turn means "fight."

Feral Females

The most notorious and high-profile London girl gangs are the Shower Gyals (Tottenham), PYG (Peckham), and OCS (Brixton). Last year a running feud between the PYG (who sport a uniform of black bandanas) and OCS erupted into a street fight in Camberwell New Road which resulted in one girl being thrown to the ground and stamped on. Some of the gang members were only 12 years old.

More recently, an eco-activist and documentary maker named Franny Armstrong was menaced near her house in Camden by a bunch of jeering 11-year-olds mumbling vague threats and brandishing a long metal bar. Armstrong was fortunate. She called for help

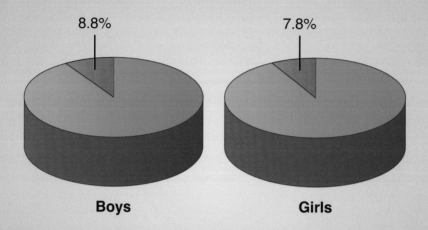

Percentage of Boys and Girls in Europe Who Claim to Be Gang Members

8.8%

7.8%

Boys

Girls

Taken from: F. Esbenson, B.T. Brick, C. Melde, et al., "The Role of Race and Ethnicity in Gang Membership," in *Street Gangs, Migration and Ethnicity*, edited by F. Van Gemert et al., 2008.

from a passer-by and was bizarrely 'rescued' by none other than Boris Johnson, who was cycling past. The Mayor of London immediately leapt off his saddle and her 'knight on shining bicycle' successfully gave chase to the 'bitches', shouting 'You oiks!' What a local hero: Bojo turned Rambo.

However, for the innocent young mother out shopping in Wembley last Friday afternoon [November 6, 2009] with her two-year-old toddler, 'RamBojo' was sadly not about. She was senselessly attacked by two teenage girls, who after failing in their attempt to rob her, punched her baby in the face before fleeing.

Recession rage, Broken Britain and the rise of binge-drinking can't quite shoulder all the blame for this 'feral female' phenomenon. The behaviour of these kids is more likely to be rooted in the fact that they feel totally forgotten. Misplaced. Abandoned. Predominately the product of dysfunctional and fractured families, they feel worthless, unloved and devoid of hope. They roam their dystopian, sink-estate wastelands like evil avatars of their own imagination. Their DNA has short-circuited and has undone them. When nurture cocks up—or is all but nonexistent—nature in its most primal form takes over:

it's a warped form of self-protection. Look to the mother. If she has failed to provide a positive role model and has barely bothered with the most basic mothering skills, are we really surprised that we are now seeing the dark side of femininity asserting itself? As one gang member was recently quoted as saying, 'My Mum works all the time so I hardly ever get to see her, and there is no one at home, so I don't feel I have anyone looking after me.'

Perhaps the weaker sex never intended to show all this strength. Perhaps the girls just need to be loved.

EVALUATING THE AUTHOR'S ARGUMENTS:

Sarah Standing opens her essay with a personal anecdote about her daughter's harrowing encounter with a gang of girls. Identify the other kinds of evidence she uses to support her argument that British girl gangs are becoming a "nationwide epidemic." Do you find this evidence persuasive? Why or why not?

The Problem of Girls in Gangs Has Been Overstated

"[The] horror stories about girl gangs . . . are strikingly short on hard evidence but long on hair-raising interviews with kids."

Joan Smith

In the following viewpoint Joan Smith disputes the claim that a growing number of London girls are joining criminal gangs. She believes that the media have exaggerated and overdramatized the issue of girl gang membership, noting that news reports about these gangs are often based on personal anecdotes rather than strong evidence. Moreover, she notes, media hype about "girl gangsters" is dangerous because it both glamorizes gangs and mislabels groups that are not gangs. Smith is a columnist, critic, novelist, and human rights activist.

AS YOU READ, CONSIDER THE FOLLOWING QUESTIONS:
1. What is the solution to gang violence, in the author's opinion?
2. How many female gangs are there in London, according to the Metropolitan Police and as cited in the viewpoint?
3. How might young people react to adults' anxiety about youth gangs, in Smith's view?

It's a bit like watching the trailer for that hilarious sci-fi classic, *Attack of the 50 Ft Woman*, which thrilled audiences with the news that "the most grotesque monstrosity of all" was on the loose. This time, to be fair, the monsters are the same size as the rest of us but the really terrible thing about them, like the deranged avenger in that Fifties movie, is their sex.

"Girls are killing guys", a young man declared on yesterday morning's [August 22, 2007] *Today* programme. "They think girls are angels and boys are devils, but sometimes girls can be the devil", said a terrified 14-year-old girl.

Ah, those devil girls: it could only be August, a month when killer sharks are spotted off Cornwall, baby tigers pop through cat flaps and David Cameron [then a member of Parliament in the United Kingdom] promises to repeal the Human Rights Act. To be honest, I'm kicking myself; when last week's big news story was the danger of confronting teenage boys about their anti-social behaviour, I should have known that "bad girls"—as Jenni Murray memorably called them on *Woman's Hour* a couple of months ago—would not be far behind. It's happened so often that on this occasion I can't even be bothered to misquote [Rudyard] Kipling on the female of the species being deadlier than the male.

A Failed Media Attempt at "Balance"

It's one of the iron rules of a misogynistic culture that any story about men or boys behaving badly has to be followed by a "balancing" piece in which someone points out that women and girls are pretty awful too. This is not to suggest I don't think there's a problem with adolescent boys and anti-social behaviour, especially after two tragic deaths in the space of a week, but it's important to keep things in proportion; not every boy aged between 13 and 18 is in a gang, carrying a knife or gun and looking for a confrontation to prove how tough he is.

The number of young men injured and killed in this kind of violence is unacceptable but the solution—teaching vulnerable boys to have a secure identity which isn't based on violence—is pretty obvious. At the same time, as long as this kind of brittle, showy masculinity continues to be valorised in popular cuture—and it certainly is in rap music—it's inevitable that some equally vulnerable girls will be drawn towards it.

Common sense dictates that they will be abused as a result, both sexually—being raped by gang members is not uncommon—and by being lured into criminal behaviour themselves.

It is a fact that men commit many more violent offences than women, although violent women—because they offend cultural notions about women being the "nurturing" sex—tend to get heavier sentences; when taboos are broken, people are horrified and excited in about equal measure, something that's worth bearing in mind whenever the subject of female violence returns to the agenda.

Not Much Hard Evidence

This week's horror stories about girl gangs are a perfect example; they are strikingly short on hard evidence but long on hair-raising interviews with kids who claim to have personal experience of the phenomenon. "I can show you six or seven [girl gangs] in one area", claimed an excitable interviewee on yesterday's *Today* programme.

This would suggest that London has dozens, if not hundreds, of girl gangs rampaging through the streets and causing mayhem. Yet the Metropolitan Police is aware of a total of 170 gangs in the capital

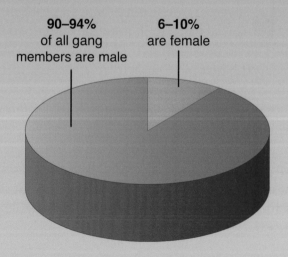

Gang Members in the United States: Male and Female

90–94%
of all gang
members are male

6–10%
are female

Taken from: www.helpinggangyouth.com.

and, of those, only three are exclusively female. This hasn't stopped the BBC [British Broadcasting Corporation] returning to the subject throughout the summer, with *Woman's Hour* and a *Radio 1* documentary entitled "Mean Girls" blazing the trail for yesterday's *Today* investigation. "Shock! Frenzy! Devastation!" Sorry, I'm talking about *Attack of the 50 Ft Woman* again, although there's clearly no shortage of kids in 2007 who are willing to tell reporters about muggings and robberies they have witnessed or taken part in.

Such claims are impossible to verify, especially when the interviewees are identified only by a first name; some of them sound very much like teenage bragging. What is needed to justify all these colourful claims is some statistics, and they have been noticeably

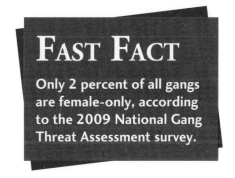

FAST FACT

Only 2 percent of all gangs are female-only, according to the 2009 National Gang Threat Assessment survey.

absent. "A BBC investigation for the *Today* programme has found that an increasing number of girls are operating in gangs, some as young as seven", James Naughtie declared yesterday, yet the report which followed offered no hard evidence for the proposition. Naughtie suggested that girl gangs are "prevalent", which certainly doesn't match my experience.

Two months earlier, there was a surreal discussion on *Woman's Hour* which simply assumed that girl gangs were a growing problem. Jenni Murray, usually the most sensible of interviewers, asked how this situation had come about and what should be done without ever establishing that the problem really existed.

The item was prompted by a real event, the fatal stabbing of a girl in Croydon a week earlier which was said to have followed an argument between the victim and a girl gang, and the programme claimed there had been "an increase in reported incidents of girls' involvement in gang violence".

Once again, this is an imprecise formulation which could mean one of several things—that more girls are being drawn into boys' gangs, as girlfriends for instance, or that there has been an increase in girls forming their own gangs.

London police prepare to raid a gang house in 2011. The Metropolitan Police say that out of 170 gangs in London only 3 are exclusively female.

Mislabeling Groups Is Dangerous

Susannah Hancock, London regional manager of the Youth Justice Board, thought the first explanation was more likely, telling Murray that boys' gangs were getting younger and that more girls were becoming involved on the periphery—to carry drugs, for instance. She emphasised the danger of classifying any identifiable group of girls as a gang, a point which shouldn't need making given the propensity of girls down the ages to form close friendship groups without necessarily involving themselves in anything worse than sharing lipstick.

Three months ago, the Youth Justice Board addressed the subject of young people's involvement in gangs and stressed the importance of making a distinction between "real" gangs and groups of young people who may commit low-level anti-social behaviour. "Mislabelling of youth groups as gangs runs the risk of glamourising them and may even encourage young people to become invoved in more serious criminal behaviour," it warned.

This is a real danger, and one of the few sensible observations that's been made about the subject in recent months.

Another danger is that we start seeing "gangs" on every corner, further alienating kids who are suspicious of adults but haven't yet got involved in criminal behaviour. I'm still no wiser about the number of girls involved in gangs, but you'll have to excuse me while I check my windows—I just can't stop thinking about that 50-foot woman.

EVALUATING THE AUTHOR'S ARGUMENTS:

Joan Smith contends that the media have exaggerated the problem of girls joining gangs in London. She disagrees with the author of the previous viewpoint, Sarah Standing, who claims that British girl gangs are a significant, and growing, problem. Which author presents a more credible argument, in your opinion? Explain your answer.

Responding to Gangs in the School Setting

Michelle Arciaga, Wayne Sakamoto, and Errika Fearbry Jones

"Some of the most dangerous gang activities in any community may take place in and around local schools."

According to the authors of the following viewpoint, an increasing number of students are reporting the presence of gangs in American public schools. However, school administrators often deny that their school has a gang problem—possibly because they do not recognize gang activity when it occurs or because acknowledging a gang problem would make it seem like they are failing at their job. Those schools that do openly respond to gang problems through awareness and prevention efforts increase the level of safety and security in their communities, the authors note. Michelle Arciaga is a senior research associate with the National Gang Center in Tallahassee, Florida. Wayne Sakamoto is the director of school safety for the Murrieta Valley Unified School District in Murrieta, California. Errika Fearbry Jones is the coordinator of the Teaching and Learning Environment for the School District of Pittsburgh, Pennsylvania.

1. What percent of students in public schools have reported the presence of gangs and gang members at school, according to the authors?
2. According to a 2001 survey, as cited in the viewpoint, what percentage of secondary level students claimed to be members of a gang?
3. What percentage of school principals has reported a gang presence in their schools, according to data cited by the authors?

G angs are present in many schools in the United States. The *National Survey of American Attitudes on Substance Abuse XV: Teens and Parents*, released in August 2010 by the National Center on Addiction and Substance Abuse, reported that:

Forty-five percent of high school students say that there are gangs or students who consider themselves to be part of a gang in their schools.

Thirty-five percent of middle-school students say that there are gangs or students who consider themselves to be part of a gang in their schools.

The differences between public and private schools are stark. While 46 percent of students in public schools reported the presence of gangs and gang members at school, only 2 percent of private school students did.

A Growing Gang Presence on Urban Campuses

According to the School Crime Supplement to the National Crime Victimization Survey (2007), 23 percent of students reported the presence of gangs on their school campus or in the surrounding area in 2007. This represents an increase in the percentage of students reporting gangs on/around campus in 2003 (21 percent). Schools in urban areas appear to be the most affected by the presence of gangs: 36 percent of urban students reported gangs, versus 21 percent of suburban and 16 percent of rural students in 2005.

In a survey of students conducted in almost 1,300 schools nationwide, 7.6 percent of male respondents and 3.8 percent of female respondents at the secondary level reported that they belonged to a gang. Based on the increased number of students reporting a gang presence at school between 2001 and 2010, this number has likely increased, although no subsequent nationwide studies have been conducted.

Gang members do not leave their conflicts, attitudes, and behaviors outside the school doors. Some of the most dangerous gang activities in any community may take place in and around local schools. Gang members encounter each other at school during class changes, in the lunchroom, in common areas, and during assemblies and school events. Students may loiter on or around the school campus before and after school, and conflicts may occur between rival gangs. In some instances, gang members come to school to engage in criminal behavior (drug dealing) or to confront rivals. . . .

Why Schools May Deny Gang Problems

In some instances, schools have operated like islands in the larger community, with school administrators and staff believing they are immune to community problems or failing to recognize the signs of gang activity at school. In other instances, heavy-handed responses to gangs have pushed gang-involved youth away from school and educational opportunities, exacerbating community and individual gang problems.

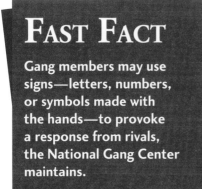

Fast Fact

Gang members may use signs—letters, numbers, or symbols made with the hands—to provoke a response from rivals, the National Gang Center maintains.

For a number of reasons, denial seems to be especially prevalent among school administrators. Although only a very small percentage of principals (5 percent) reported the presence of gangs in their schools, more than one-third (36 percent) reported the presence of gangs in the immediate community. Interestingly enough, this study reports that "in the 10 percent of schools with the highest student gang participation rates (14.4 percent or more of students reporting gang participation), only 18 percent of the principals" reported the presence of gangs.

There are many reasons that school personnel may not acknowledge the existence of gangs.

School-wide gang prevention efforts include gang awareness, dress-code policies, classroom management, and talking to mentors and role models.

First, in many cases, school staff and administrators do not recognize gang activity when they see it. Training and preparation are crucial to an effective response to gangs in the learning environment.

Second, for many school administrators, public admission that the school has a population of gang members might seem like a failure to properly control the school climate. It is important for school administrators to realize that there is no shame attached to the presence of gang members in school. The only shame lies in failing to adequately prepare for or address the needs of gang-involved students.

Third, school-choice laws that have been passed in many areas make it possible for parents to remove their children from a particular school. Schools with a reputation for having a gang problem can lose students. Other negative ramifications for school administrators and the school itself may include loss of funding due to population decreases. However, failing to adequately address gang problems can lead to increased risk of victimization in the school setting for both students and staff members. Schools must walk the fine line between overreacting to the gang problem and attempting to hide or downplay it.

Dos and Don'ts for School Personnel

DO	DON'T
Do treat gang-involved students with the same respect and value shown to other students.	**Do not** humiliate or embarrass gang-involved students (especially in front of peers).
Do have high expectations for academic achievement.	**Do not** publicly praise a gang member for academic achievement before checking with the student.
Do expect gang-involved students to submit assignments.	**Do not** allow students to write gang symbols or turn in assignments with gang-style writing.
Do provide more cooperative and hands-on learning experiences.	**Do not** allow gang members from the same set to work together.
Do actively involve gang members in the learning process.	**Do not** allow gang-involved students to "disappear" in the classroom.
Do talk to students individually about gang involvement.	**Do not** allow your classroom to be used as a gang forum.
Do enlist gang-involved students to work with other students on school projects and other extracurricular activities.	**Do not** allow students to form cliques and exclude other groups.
Do set definite rules and consequences. Suspend, file charges, etc., if warranted. Gang members respect and expect discipline and structure.	**Do not** change your mind about enforcing rules. Gang members view inconsistency as a weakness and will exploit it.
Do enforce all rules with respect.	**Do not** challenge or try to intimidate gang-involved youth, especially in front of their peers.
Do provide consequences for **ALL** students.	**Do not** make exceptions for favorite students.
Do stay current on words or activities that are gang-related: dress, rap music, hair nets, etc.	**Do not** allow students to use words or activities that are gang-related.
Do know students by street names or nicknames.	**Do not** allow students to refer to each other by gang monikers.
Do give gang members responsibility that enhances their positive self-esteem: tutors, helpers, etc.	**Do not** trust gang members completely. Be a guide and a mentor, not a peer.
Do show concern and empathy for gang-involved youth.	**Do not** become an enabler by providing excuses for students' negative behaviors.
Do keep communication with gang-involved youth informal, open, and honest.	**Do not** become a home boy/girl to gang members.

Taken from: Michelle Arciaga, Wayne Sakamoto, Errika Fearbry Jones. "Responding to Gangs in the School Setting," *National Gang Center Bulletin*, November 2010.

Finally, schools may be reluctant to share information on gang activity in and around the school for fear of violating confidentiality laws. In most cases, this is also a training issue. Schools can legally share information on gang-involved students across agency boundaries with a number of key agencies, including law enforcement and juvenile probation/parole. Schools also have a responsibility to continually share information on policies and procedures relating to gangs with parents and students. In addition, schools and law enforcement can and should share information about gang-related incidents involving students on campus or in the community. This shared information can help these entities prevent further acts of retaliation and violence.

Most schools and school districts that have openly addressed gang problems have found that students and staff members, as well as parents and the community, are safer and feel more secure. . . .

School-Based Gang Prevention

Schoolwide gang prevention efforts include . . . gang awareness, classroom management, dress-code policies, and provision of mentors and role models. Prevention efforts could include:

- Providing students with skills and knowledge to help them avoid gang involvement. For example, schools may opt to utilize the Gang Resistance Education And Training (G.R.E.A.T.) program, in which trained law enforcement officers provide skills-based classroom lessons in elementary and middle schools. G.R.E.A.T. officers and deputies also may provide summer activities and a family-strengthening curriculum.
- Implementing after-school activities that provide youth with opportunities to become involved with positive groups and to develop skills that will allow them to stay out of gangs. These programs offer youth structured and skills-based programming during critical times when many youth may be unsupervised and on the streets. After-school programs are an opportunity to extend the school day and provide additional academic support and development. Research has indicated that early academic success is a protective factor against gangs and delinquent behaviors. After-school programs also offer an opportunity for youth to bond with positive role models and learn new social-emotional

skills. The Boys & Girls Clubs of America utilize a "targeted prevention" approach that identifies youth who may be at high risk of gang involvement because of a number of risk factors, including gang involvement by other family members. These youth are targeted or selected for involvement in prevention efforts through after-school programs in many areas. This approach also could be replicated by school staff and paraprofessionals in areas where such programs are not available.

• Involving parents in gang prevention efforts. Schools may serve as hubs where parents are trained in gang awareness and strategies to keep their children out of gangs. Parents also may be recruited to protect the safety of students in and around the school campus simply by being visibly present before, after, and during school hours. One such program, Parents on Patrol, places trained parents at critical places in the community where they report any problems or safety concerns to the school or law enforcement. Many students must walk home through gang territories, where they may become targets of the local gang, or are driven to the gang out of fear and the need for protection. Safe-passage programs offer support, supervision, and protection for these youth to and from school and give parents or community members ownership in gang prevention and safety.

EVALUATING THE AUTHOR'S ARGUMENTS:

The authors of this viewpoint contend that administrators and principals are often in denial about the presence of gangs in their schools. Contact your local public school district to see if there are any current policies on gang awareness and prevention. According to what you have read in this viewpoint and elsewhere in this text, do you think that your district needs to revise or update its policies on gangs? Why or why not?

Gangs Are a Growing Problem in the Suburbs

"Gang membership in America has been stretching out from the inner cities . . . into such places as small town Wisconsin."

Mary Ellen Flannery

Gangs are not solely an inner-city issue, writes Mary Ellen Flannery in the following viewpoint. A growing number of suburban youths are joining gangs, although many school districts do not want to admit that they have a gang problem. Moreover, after many schools banned gang identifiers such as colored bandannas, youths have found new ways to broadcast gang membership, including baseball caps, tattoos, and beads, notes Flannery. Some teachers maintain that the problem of gangs in the suburbs is overstated—and that there are many more "wannabe" gangsters than actual criminals in their schools. But experts warn that vigilance and awareness are necessary in the current climate. Flannery is a writer and editor for the National Education Association in Washington, DC.

AS YOU READ, CONSIDER THE FOLLOWING QUESTIONS:
  1. How many youths are members of gangs, according to the US Justice Department and as cited by the author?
  2. What are the two major gang alliances in the United States, according to Flannery?
  3. According to Javier Castellanos, as quoted by the author, what does an "MOB" tattoo signify?

Y ou may not think you have gang members in your school. You may think that your students aren't those kinds of kids. Maybe you think they're too rich, too suburban, too smart, or too White.

Think again.

"If you don't think you have a gang problem, you're in the wrong business," says Detective Javier Castellanos, a New Jersey gang specialist in a recent training for school staff in northern New Jersey.

"You do," he adds firmly.

"We know it!" says a voice from the back.

From the Cities to the Suburbs

For decades, gang membership in America has been stretching out from the inner cities of Los Angeles, Chicago, and New York, into such places as small town Wisconsin. Past the gates in South Florida's cul-de-sac communities, into the big houses of Washington, D.C.'s suburbs, even down the street from the Billy Graham Center in the most churched-up town in this country, you will find boys and girls in gangs. And that means you'll find them in your schools, too.

According to the most recent U.S. Justice Department surveys, somewhere around 750,000 kids are hanging, fighting, and pushing drugs in 24,000 different gangs. In 2000, 95 percent of law enforcement respondents "identified (gang) activity within one or more of the high schools in their jurisdictions. Ninety-one percent reported gang activity within one or more intermediate schools."

Since then, according to the 2004 National Youth Gang Survey, about half of the surveyed agencies say things have gotten better or stayed the same, but the other half say it's even bloodier than before. At the same time, the federal data collectors say their numbers, which rely on reports from local police, may not provide an accurate accounting. Not surprisingly, not all want to admit they have a gang problem. It's not such a great thing for property values, notes Castellanos dryly.

And not all school districts want to admit it either.

"What constitutes a problem?" asks a suburban Connecticut high school teacher. "Our district has gangs—but we're in denial."

A History Lesson

Castellanos and his partners in the Passaic County [New Jersey] Sheriff's Department have perfected a Rambo-style, take-no-prisoners presentation on youth gangs that leaves at least one school nurse wiping tears off her cheek and a few veteran truant officers shaking their heads. "I've been in that kid's house," whispers one, as the detective clicks past a PowerPoint slide of a bullet-scarred teenager.

"You ever hear a kid go 'Bla-a-a-a-att!' like simulated gunfire, when he's walking into your classroom?" Castellanos asks.

"Oh my God. I hear that!"

Police tape marks the spot were five people were shot at a rally at the Texas Southern University campus in July 2009. Rival gangs from Houston and Fresno, Texas, were responsible, according to police.

"And then, if you get another one answering 'Suuu-wooo! you'd better duck!" Castellanos says. The first is a popular East Coast Bloods greeting, while the latter is pure West Coast.

Ready for a history lesson?

Basically, there are two major gang alliances in the United States: Folk Nation and People Nation. Within those alliances are the actual gangs (in the same way that the American League includes the Yankees and Red Sox). The Folk Nation, for example, boasts of big names like the Los Angeles-based Crips and Chicago-based Gangster Disciples. Within the People Nation are the Bloods and Latin Kings.

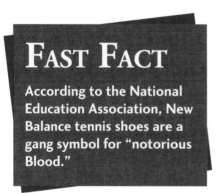

FAST FACT

According to the National Education Association, New Balance tennis shoes are a gang symbol for "notorious Blood."

Each gang has its own set of identifiers. Remember the big deal about bandannas in schools? You'd see a kid draped in red scarves, tied around their heads and legs, and know they belonged—or wanted to look like they belonged—to a chapter of Bloods. In response, many schools have banned them. But the kids have moved on. There are new ways to signal affiliation.

"You see a kid with a jacket hanging on their left shoulder—they're telling you they're Folk Nation, could be Crip," Castellanos warns. They might pull their left pocket out, roll up their left pant leg, or wear their belt buckle to the left. Regular baseball caps are very big. Why are all the kids in one New Jersey project wearing Pittsburgh Steelers caps? Because the team's colors also are Latin Kings colors. Why are other East Coast kids wearing Kansas City Chiefs caps?

Because "KC means "Kill Crips."

Tattoos are telling, too. Don't believe the kid who tells you that his "MOB" tattoo means "man of business," or "money over bitches," Castellanos says. It means "member of Bloods." Or look for strands of colored beads, sometimes modified rosaries, which are popular among the most faithful gang members.

The other day, Castellanos, who has moved from New Jersey to a wooded suburb of Pennsylvania, ran into an obvious Bloods member in his local grocery store. "The salad dressing aisle!" he recalls with amazement. The street-wise officer flashed a few elaborate hand signals, shouted, "What's poppin', dawg?" and the gang member greeted him with delight: "You Blood?"

"Nah, man. I'm a cop."

Keep Ya Head Up

How far does the detective have to move his two daughters? Is there a nice little town where boys don't get "beat in" and girls don't get "sexed in"?

He doesn't think so. "Gangs go everywhere," he says, (He just got a photo of gang-related graffiti in Afghanistan.) His colleagues in law enforcement, all over the United States, see the same problems. "We've had gangs in Northern Virginia for some years, for the most part in the inner suburbs," says Leesburg, Virginia, Chief of Police Joe Price. "In the early parts of this decade, we saw it moving to the outer suburbs, which is happening all over the country."

Price is co-chair of a regional taskforce that involves everybody from the Secret Service to the local school board—and it shares credit for reining in the rapid expansion of MS-13, a fast-growing, machete-wielding Central American gang. The task force also has trained every teacher in its region, much like the New Jersey team. (In New Jersey, teacher training in gang awareness is required by state law, and Castellanos is a regular guest at New Jersey Education Association-sponsored conferences.)

"One of the worst things that a community can do is put its head in the sand and say it doesn't have a problem," Price says. "Gangs will develop so rapidly that by the time they're forced to realize it, it's too late."

But all this red-button talk about gang-bangers in the suburbs—doesn't it all seem a little over the top? Just because a kid starts flashing shadow puppets with his hands, does it mean he's dealing dope? If he talks [deceased American rapper] Tupac [Shakur] does it mean he's smacking his classmates after school? "Kids pose. They want to pretend to be part of something," says Josh Ajima, a teacher at Dominion High School in Northern Virginia.

Many classroom teachers say that they're overwhelmed with "wannabes," who are definitely annoying, but not necessarily illegal. By definition, a gang member must be engaged in criminal activity.

"I can't stand people who tap-dance around problems and say there is no problem. But I think this is such an over-dramatized issue," says Pam Smith, a Northern Virginia teacher with 20-plus years of experience. Smith had a student recently suspended for two weeks for spraying "gang-related" graffiti in school. "He's a great kid, so naïve. He's as much a gang member as my 80-year-old mother!"

The Need for Vigilance

But Emily Tusin tells a different story. Tusin, a second-year elementary teacher in suburban Wheaton, Illinois, home to the Billy Graham Center and the most churches per capita in America, knows she had a gang member in her classroom last year [2007]. "He was a new kid and he came in with notches in his eyebrow to show he was a member of a gang. He came right in, saw another kid—who he didn't know—and he actually punched that kid in the face because he was wearing the wrong color."

Both Smith and Tusin are likely right. Would-be gangsters are walking around on campuses, as are the real deal. What's important is to learn the difference. "Keep your eyes and ears open. If you get any kind of inkling that a young person is involved in gang activity—gang graffiti on their notebook, they're wearing colors, hats—talk to your local police," advises Wheaton Deputy Chief Tom Meloni.

"It might be nothing more than a comic book club, but the best course of action is to be vigilant," he says. "The more you tolerate, the worse it gets. And once they get entrenched, they're very difficult to eradicate. I worked in South Central L.A.—I know!"

Gangster 4 Life

Once a kid gets into a gang, there are basically two ways out: the back of a police car or a hearse, Castellanos says. "Unless a parent has the resources to pack up and move, there really aren't any options," he adds.

Prevention is the key. If you're a parent, get your child's MySpace password, he urges. Gangs do recruitment and organization on social networking sites. He's not a big fan of gangster rap. Nor does he care much for gang-related video games, like the Grand Theft Auto series.

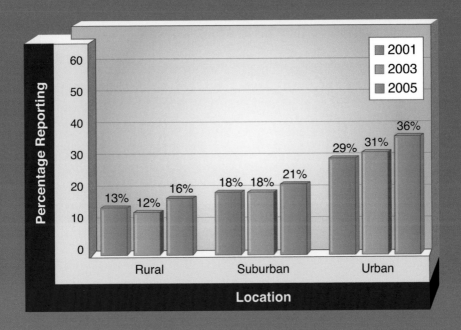

Percentage of Students Reporting Gang Activity at Schools

Taken from: "Gang Proliferation." www.justice.gov.

"Would you let a sex offender in your house? Would you invite a gang member into your house? That's what you're doing when you buy these games for your kids."

Ask your kids where they're going, who they're going with, and what time they'll be home. Most of all, as parents and educators, seek out ways to spend time with kids and involve them in after-school activities, he says.

Dan Korem, the Dallas-based author of *Suburban Gangs: The Affluent Rebels*, has found success with a prevention program that partners at-risk kids with "protectors," usually teachers. That person promises to call the student every week and stop by twice a month. "How could an hour have so much impact?" Korem asks. "Because so many kids don't have anybody in their corner. That small amount of time has an out-of-proportion impact."

Kids join gangs for a variety of reasons—including money and access to drugs—but the primary one shared by members in inner-cities, suburbs, and country towns is this: A sense of belonging.

"When you go into some of these homes and see the way these kids live—they have everything they want!" Castellanos says. "But they don't have everything they need, which is love."

EVALUATING THE AUTHOR'S ARGUMENTS:

Identify the elements of description, dialogue, and narrative in Mary Ellen Flannery's article. Do these elements engage you as a reader? Do you think her style of writing makes her argument more compelling? Explain.

Chapter 2

What Causes Gang Violence?

Police investigate a gang-related shooting in Brownsville, Brooklyn, New York, on October 21, 2011. The main factors driving gang memberships are the illegal drug trade and poverty.

North America's Demand for Illegal Drugs Fosters Gang Violence

"Recent gang violence in Vancouver [British Columbia, Canada, is] linked directly to the [Mexican drug] cartels."

Globe and Mail

In the following viewpoint the editors of Toronto, Canada's daily *Globe and Mail* newspaper maintain that the illegal drug trade is a serious threat to the security of the Western Hemisphere. They contend that drug trafficking, fueled by North America's unending demand for banned substances, sparks violent conflicts among gangs, local criminal groups, and organized crime networks. In the authors' view, the Canadian government should devote much more energy and resources to the war on drugs.

AS YOU READ, CONSIDER THE FOLLOWING QUESTIONS:

1. What is the mission of the American Police Community, according to the editors of the *Globe and Mail?*
2. About how many of the drug cartels' guns come from the United States, according to the author?
3. Which illegal drugs are known to be produced in Canada?

It is convenient to think of the drug wars as a peculiarly Mexican problem, focused on the border Mexico shares with the U.S. It isn't. The drug trade has become a grave threat to hemispheric security. And the Canadian government has not fully grasped the seriousness of the problem.

Mexico's drug-trafficking organizations are the undisputed jefes of the region, with distribution lines from the streets of Buenos Aires to Vancouver. Drug-trafficking organizations are destabilizing not just Mexico, but many other parts of Latin America, and the Caribbean. Crime has become the number one concern in all countries in the region, according to a 2010 Latinobarometro poll. Canada too has felt the full force of their power, with recent gang violence in Vancouver linked directly to the cartels.

Police in Vancouver, British Columbia, remove a body following a gang-related shooting. Vancouver has been called Canada's gang capital because Mexican drug cartels have infiltrated the area.

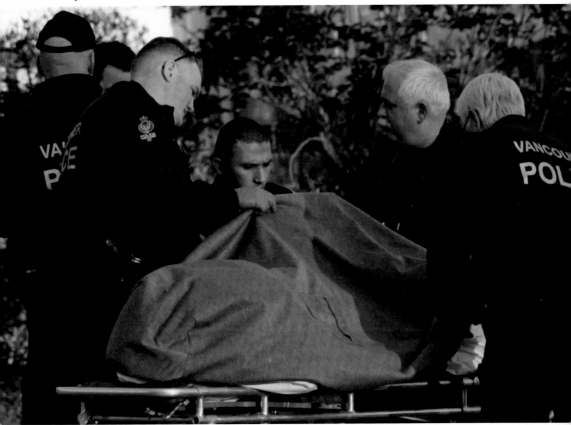

Central America's death toll from violence is as high as it was at the peak of the civil wars. Last year, there were more homicides in Guatemala and Honduras together than in the European Union's 27 countries combined, as indigenous criminal groups wage a battle with the cartels, pushed south by Mexican President Felipe Calderon's military campaign against them. Drug-trafficking organizations have also established transport routes through the Caribbean. Their activity has reached "major cities in the entire continental U.S., as well as some major cities in Canada," according to the U.S. Drug Enforcement Administration.

Canada has failed to recognize the extent to which security in the hemisphere is being undermined by these highly mobile, vertically integrated transnational criminal groups.

In May Canada signed an anti-organized-crime agreement with Mexico, agreeing to assist with police training and justice reform. Yet Ottawa has dispatched only eight RCMP officers, and directed just $4-million to strengthen the country's judiciary. It has chosen to be an observer of, rather than a direct participant in, the newly launched American Police Community—a hemispheric police organization whose prime mission is to fight the drug cartels.

FAST FACT

The United Nations reports that there are an estimated 250 million drug users worldwide.

This inactivity is especially puzzling given Prime Minister Stephen Harper's oft-stated goal to help build a more prosperous, democratic and secure Latin America and Caribbean.

"Canada has a future in working with the two American neighbours to fight a common, corrosive and growing threat to all of our societies," Admiral James Winnefield, head of the U.S. Northern Command and the NORAD defence pact, said during a recent visit to Toronto.

The demand for cocaine, heroin and methamphetamines in the U.S., and Canada, fuels the trade. The U.S.—source of some 60,000 guns that have armed the cartels—has recognized its role. Washington's $1.6-billion Plan Merida is directed toward helping Mexico with intelligence, training and the rebuilding of communities

plagued by drug violence. It is likely only a fraction of what the U.S. will need to spend.

Why does Canada remain largely on the sidelines? Though a much smaller drug market, cocaine use has actually increased in Canada in the last decade. Canada is also a robust producer of methamphetamines and marijuana, and a natural draw for cocaine distributors wishing to trade in kind.

Canada needs to view the drug trade for what it really is: a global criminal threat driven by an apparently insatiable demand for drugs in North America.

"Drugs are the AIDS of Latin America," says Johanna Mendelson, with the Center for Strategic and International Studies in Washington. "An epidemic killing innocent people."

Canada is not immune. In British Columbia, Mexican drug cartels enjoy operational ties with the province's drug distributors, says Constable Michael McLaughlin, with the RCMP's federal drug enforcement branch. Though local biker gangs still run the drug trade, the RCMP have intercepted $13-million in cocaine in three different busts in the past two months, and two of the cases have direct connections to Mexican drug cartels.

U.S. Secretary of State Hillary Clinton has mused that parts of Mexico are in danger of becoming a narco-state. If that happens, Canada will be affected in myriad ways. Canada has three times more direct foreign investment in Latin America than it does with Asia, and does $25-billion in annual bilateral trade with Mexico. Every year, more than 1.2 million Canadian tourists visit Mexico. "Mexico is an important export and investment market," says Jennifer Jeffs, president of the Canadian International Council. "It is in our interests that it remains a thriving and functional democracy."

Organized criminal drug networks are a serious and growing threat to the stability of the Americas. Canada is an integral part of the problem—and the region—and must play a greater role in the solution. It should begin by joining the hemispheric policing association, work more closely with Mexico City and Washington and put its heart (and more resources) into the struggle.

EVALUATING THE AUTHOR'S ARGUMENTS:

In this viewpoint the editors of the *Globe and Mail* contend that North American street gangs have connections to drug-trafficking organizations and transnational criminal groups, and that the drug trade is a serious threat to the Western Hemisphere. How should this threat be confronted, in their opinion? Do you think their proposals would be effective? Why or why not?

The War on Drugs Fosters Gang Violence

"The proliferation of gangs over the last four decades is a direct result of President [Richard] Nixon's declared war on drugs."

James Murr

The strict ban on certain drugs in the United States has led to the large increase in gangs during the past few decades, writes James Murr in the following viewpoint. He contends that gangs would lose their major source of income if drugs were legalized. Then, funds allocated to build prisons and punish drug users could instead be used to support after-school programs for at-risk youths. Murr is a resident of Santa Maria, California, who worked in probation in the 1970s and early 1980s.

AS YOU READ, CONSIDER THE FOLLOWING QUESTIONS:

1. According to Murr, about how many drug-trafficking gangs have moved to the United States from Latin America?
2. What percentage of the US prison population has been charged with drug-related offenses, according to Cornell University and as cited by the author?
3. In the author's opinion, why do youths join gangs?

The *Santa Maria Times* has published numerous letters regarding gangs in Santa Maria. Most of them are on target, but some blame the Police Department for not doing more to suppress them.

When I worked for the Probation Department back in the 1970s and early 1980s, gangs were very different. The main difference is that the war on drugs actually fueled gangs, as trafficking increased. Drug money from U.S. residents is massive.

It is estimated that more than 250 drug gangs have moved in from Latin America to establish pipelines from the drug source. Smaller local gangs are also involved in illegal drug distribution.

The proliferation of gangs over the last four decades is a direct result of President Nixon's declared war on drugs. The continuation has proven this war as the biggest failed social experiment in history. We cannot seem to end it the way prohibition of alcohol was ended, when alcohol distributors were licensed.

As a nation, as well as locally, we allow ourselves to use legally two powerful drugs—alcohol and tobacco. Tobacco is as addictive as cocaine or heroin, and it kills about a half-million citizens annually. Why is the situation so convoluted where some drugs are legal and others are not?

Eighty percent of the US prison population is incarcerated for drug-related offenses.

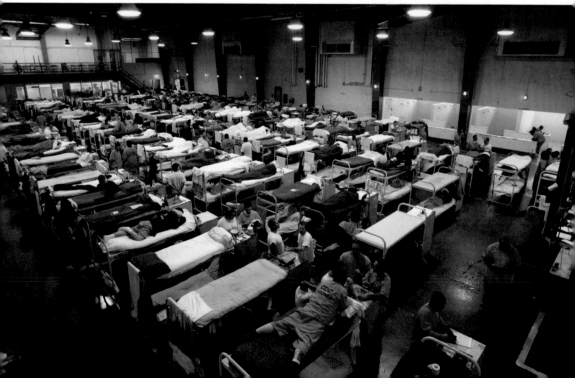

The prison industrial complex in California is swamping the state budget. Locally, the county jail is perpetually overcrowded. More locals are caught up every day using or trafficking in drugs.

In 1998, Cornell University reviewed inmate population nation-wide and determined that 80 percent of inmates had drug charges against them. The nation lost the war in the planning phase, and now the U.S. is a gangster nation.

A rational argument concludes that legalizing drugs will cut off a central funding source for gangs.

Another idea was detailed by the *Times* about expanding after-school programs. The money saved by not building prisons and releasing drug users could easily fund after-school programs.

Programs could employ college students to come onto campuses to assist students with homework, athletic programs or fine arts. A few teachers could be paid over-time to assign and direct the college students.

Keeping youth occupied after school is a very good idea, because in most families both parents work. Single parents are in that bind, and all of the children become latchkey kids when no one is at home after school. Young people need lots of structure and adults watching them.

> ## FAST FACT
>
> The retail value of drugs coming into the United States is $50 billion–$100 billion each year, according to the Cato Institute.

The goal of our community and country should be to end the war on drugs and spend the money locally for engaging our youth and keeping them off of the streets.

Every youth wants to belong to something, but without clear direction, they end up connecting with people who have criminal motives. Being recruited into a gang is similar to substitute family.

Young people need to have a sense of belonging to a group. If all the young people were in after-school programs, then more youth would have a sense of community. We do not need youth hanging out on street corners without any purpose.

People will use substances, whether or not it is legal. We have built too many myths about drugs that are not true. A sound bite like "gateway drug" is political blather. That is similar to saying drinking a beer leads to alcoholism.

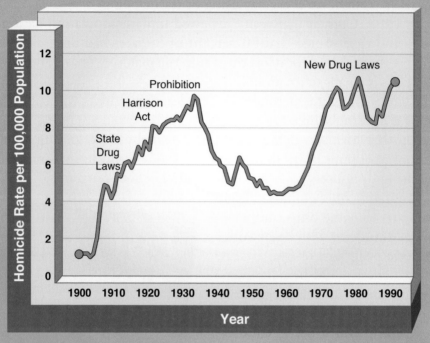

Rates for Homicides from 1900 to 1990

Homicide Rate per 100,000 Population vs. Year

State Drug Laws
Harrison Act
Prohibition
New Drug Laws

Taken from: Vital Statistics of the United States, Annual, "Historical Statistics: Colonial Times to 1970, " Series H 971-986, druglibrary.org.

We have to tune out the nonsensical propaganda and get real about our society. We have to change direction and let those who use drugs other than tobacco or alcohol be allowed to do so. We must end our gangster nation.

EVALUATING THE AUTHOR'S ARGUMENTS:

James Murr maintains that antidrug laws have created a black market that fuels the growth of street gangs. He believes that legalizing drugs would help to stop this growth. Do you agree that drug legalization would be an effective antigang strategy? Why or why not?

Poverty Fosters Gang Violence

Kai Wright

"Gang violence is intensifying because the poverty here is getting worse."

Since 2001 northeast Brooklyn's homicide rate has been climbing, despite an overall decrease in murders in the New York City area. In the following viewpoint Kai Wright explores the findings of a study conducted to discover the reasons for the murder spike in four Brooklyn precincts. The authors of the study found that the large entrenched gangs of the 1980s and 1990s have been replaced by dozens of clannish "mini-gangs" made up of armed young people who fight over drug-dealing turf and personal issues. Some contend, moreover, that a higher concentration of poverty in these neighborhoods creates stress that inevitably leads to conflict. Wright is a writer and editor in Brooklyn, New York. His work often appears in the *Nation,* the *Root,* and the *American Prospect.*

AS YOU READ, CONSIDER THE FOLLOWING QUESTIONS:

1. In New York City, what drove out the larger drug gangs of the 1980s and 1990s, according to Wright?
2. What happened to the best friend of Danny, the nineteen-year-old quoted in this viewpoint?
3. What was the population increase in the borough of Bushwick in 2006, according to the viewpoint's information from the Brooklyn Department of City Planning?

Twelve hours into 2007, Brownsville [a Brooklyn, New York, neighborhood] registered the city's first murder of the year—a 26-year-old man shot in the back while walking to the store. This year [2008] the neighborhood held the same unfortunate distinction: Just after 2 A.M. on New Year's Day, another 26-year-old—shot in the chest in front of a Brownsville housing project—became the city's first murder victim of 2008.

The intervening year was chaotic and violent in this pocket of Brooklyn. As the citywide murder rate was dropping to its lowest level in decades, murder was on the rise in four neighborhoods here: Brownsville, East New York, Bushwick, and Bedford-Stuyvesant [nicknamed Bed-Stuy]. Together, these adjacent police precincts in northeastern Brooklyn accounted for nearly a fifth of the city's murders and almost half the borough's. The police scanner rang out with these locales all year: a teen shot in the head in Bushwick Houses; two teens and a 21-year-old gunned down on Brownsville's Lott Avenue, the site of at least three shootings; a 16-year-old pounded with two slugs to the chest in Bed-Stuy's Tompkins Houses. On it went.

Of course, like the rest of the city, northeast Brooklyn is still phenomenally safer than it once was. Back in the early nineties, people in these neighborhoods got killed at two and three times last year's rate. "We had 765 murders in 1990; this morning it was 207," said Brooklyn District Attorney Charles Hynes, a few days before Brooklyn's final 2007 tally reached 212. Still, the murder rate here has been trending upward—with occasional fluctuations—since 2001. What is making this part of Brooklyn so resistant to the positive developments in the rest of the city? In 2003, Hynes commissioned a study to try to answer this question. "I woke up one day and said, 'I can't figure this out. We see the numbers coming down, but we see certain areas of definable levels of violence, particularly homicidal violence, and maybe we should go to academe [for answers].'"

A New Kind of Gang

What the academics found was a new kind of gang. The massive, corporate-style drug organizations of the eighties and early nineties are long gone from the streets of Brooklyn—driven out during the boom years by aggressive policing and an improved economic out-

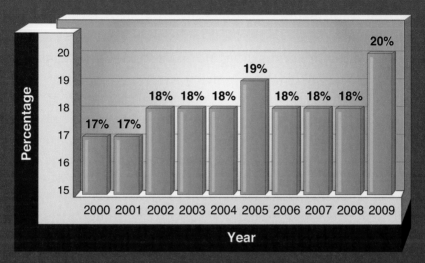

Percentage of US Children in Poverty, 2000 to 2009

look. What they left in their wake is a wildly fractured drug market populated by an amorphous and crowded field of close-knit, hard-to-identify miniature gangs—and a form of violence that may be even more difficult to tamp down than what came before it.

Names like "Crips" and "Bloods" conjure images of old-school, dyed-in-the-wool gangsters orchestrating crime through disciplined, hierarchical posses. But that's not modern New York. "These are all young kids," says Ric Curtis, chair of John Jay College of Criminal Justice's anthropology department and one of the authors of Hynes's study. "They may claim allegiance to 'Bloods,' but it's a bunch of neighborhood guys who got together and decided to call themselves Bloods."

They're still gangs, to be sure, but the label is more stylistic than organizational. The distinction's important: Instead of a couple of big gangs, there are dozens of small, clannish sets, often made up of literal cousins and next-door neighbors. Walk around Brownsville and the signs cry out from the walls. There are spray-painted B's and C's with arrows pointing upward, meaning "Bloods up" or "Crips up." But that's just the beginning. There's a laundry list of acronyms—GCC,

L*C, MAC, COCS, all groups calling themselves Crips. Northeast Brooklyn is chock-full of these mini-gangs, and they're fighting.

Personal Vendettas

The question is, what are they fighting about? Yesterday's drug violence was a means for dominating the market and protecting the product from stickup artists, who targeted street-level salesmen. Today, dealers sell primarily to known customers and avoid risky street-level sales—and, thus, should be less likely to get involved in competitive gunplay. So why all the killing? "The idea that the shootings are drug-related has some truth to it, but it's overstated," says John Jay's Greg Donaldson, who wrote a 1993 book about Brownsville and is working on a follow-up. "What they are, are people who are armed because they're in the drug trade, but then it's often personal—somebody said something to someone's girlfriend."

FAST FACT

A McClatchy newspaper analysis concluded that 16 million Americans were living in severe poverty in 2005.

That's what happened to Danny's best friend. Danny, a baby-faced 19-year-old who didn't offer his last name, has spent his whole life in Brownsville's Tilden Houses. He claims not to be in a gang, but "Crips" is scratched into the wall on his floor at Tilden—and he carries a chain of black rosary beads, which the D.A.'s office says is a gang sign that comes from prison, where guards can't confiscate religious iconography. Danny does admit to having a gun, and he's puzzled by questions about how he got it. "I took it off somebody else," he says matter of factly.

Two years ago, Danny's friend was hanging out on Rockaway Avenue, the commercial strip that runs alongside the projects, when he noticed a girl coming out of a bodega across the street. Danny's buddy hollered at her. Her boyfriend didn't like it. They argued. Danny's friend shot the other kid in the butt. He survived, but by morning, Danny's friend was dead. The 16-year-old answered a knock on the door and faced a hail of bullets. "It had to be somebody he knew or he would've never opened the door, especially after what had happened," Danny says. "He had his gun on him, but he didn't even get to pull it out."

No More Peace

Deanna Rodriguez, the D.A.'s gang-bureau chief, says the academics may be right that this sort of interpersonal beef among armed young men has caused the surge in violence in recent years. But the real concern, she argues, is that the small gangs are becoming entrenched—and starting to fight over drug-dealing turf. Maturing subsets of Latino gangs like the Latin Kings and Dominicans Don't Play, she says, are particularly worrying—which may explain the city's sharpest murder spike, in Bushwick's 83rd Precinct, where a peace between area Latin gangs has fallen part.

FBI agents escort a Latin Kings gang member after he was indicted on drug charges. Conflicts over drug dealing turf have caused a spike in the murder rates in Bushwick's 83rd precinct.

"There were several gangs that were operating in one area, and they just coexisted," says Rodriguez. "Each gang had their area, and they sold their drugs and were just able to exist independent of each other, because there was money to be made." For some reason, she says, that's broken down, and the same thing is happening all over the borough. "What appears on the surface to be a fight will have gang overtones. It's not something you readily see until you investigate it. And then you have to look at the whole area and see what's going on there."

Poverty Breeds Conflict

Ben Igwe, who runs the Family Services Network of clinics and aid agencies in Bushwick and Brownsville, believes the gang violence is intensifying because the poverty here is getting worse. The volume of food moving through his free pantry has nearly doubled in the last year, and he runs out of supplies every month. "Where are all the people who are priced out of Fort Greene and Bed-Stuy going? They come to Brownsville and Bushwick," he says. "They move in and you have this higher concentration of poverty and they are stressed— and you are going to have conflict." In 2006, Bushwick's population jumped by more than 8,000 people, or about 7 percent, according to the Department of City Planning; 13 percent of the neighborhood's residents lived in a different home than the year before. "There's a pulse," Igwe says. "You can feel it. And that stress ends in people acting out."

The Police Department has vowed to stop the acting out, and a fresh crop of academy grads started flooding into the area over the holidays. But nobody who spends time in these neighborhoods thinks the gangs will be cowed. On Christmas Eve, a 12-year-old robbery suspect escaped from a police cruiser parked at a Rockaway Avenue corner when someone just walked up and opened the car door. "People are not afraid of police, and they're not afraid of jail," says Donaldson. He acknowledges that the cops' war of attrition against organized crime brought murder rates way down at [the twentieth] century's close, but he argues no policing solution can hold permanently. "You're not dealing with the root cause," he says. "Nobody wants to hear about the root-cause thing, because it's an old story. But nobody ever gave those guys jobs."

Viewpoint

4

US Immigration Policy Fosters Gang Violence

Matthew Quirk

"For hardcore gang members, quickie deportations on immigration charges are often no more than short-term fixes."

Aggressive US deportation policies targeting Latino criminals promote gang violence, argues Matthew Quirk in the following viewpoint. When Central American gang members are deported back to their troubled home countries, they often recruit new gangsters and return to the United States, he points out. The continuing deportation-and-return cycle actually strengthens gang ties and turns small gangs into large ones. The author maintains that lengthy US prison sentences would be more effective than deportation in addressing gang violence. Quirk, a former writer for the monthly journal the *Atlantic*, is the author of *The Five Hundred*.

AS YOU READ, CONSIDER THE FOLLOWING QUESTIONS:

1. By how much did the arrests of Latino gang members increase between 2005 and 2007, according to Quirk?
2. How did MS-13 become America's "most dangerous gang," in the author's opinion?
3. According to the author, how many Central Americans are members of gangs that originated in the United States?

With anti-immigrant sentiment rising, mass deportation is making a comeback. During fiscal 2006 and 2007, the number of deportation proceedings jumped from 64,000 to 164,000. This fiscal year [2008], it is expected to hit 200,000, an all-time high.

Latino gang members have been targeted for particularly aggressive action. Since 2005, Immigration and Customs Enforcement (ICE) dragnets have swept up more than 6,000 suspected gangsters. From 2005 to 2007, arrests—usually preludes to deportation—increased more than fivefold.

How MS-13 Became an International Menace

The United States has been down this road before; the mid-1990s saw a similar wave of criminal deportations. That one helped turn a small gang from Los Angeles, Mara Salvatrucha (better known as MS-13), into an international menace and what Customs and Border Protection now calls America's "most dangerous gang." It's not clear that this one will turn out much better.

Newark, New Jersey, police director Garry McCarthy shows photos of 6 MS-13 gang members indicted on murder charges. Today, between 6,000 and 8,000 MS-13 gang members live in the United States, and membership is growing.

Gerardo Gomez   Rodolfo Godinez   Alexander Alfaro

Shahid Baskerville   Jose Carranza   Melvin Jovel

MS-13 formed in the Rampart area of Los Angeles in 1988 or 1989. A civil war in El Salvador had displaced a fifth of that country's population, and a small number of the roughly 300,000 Salvadorans living in L.A. banded together to form the gang. But MS-13 didn't really take off until several years later, in El Salvador, after the U.S. adopted a get-tough policy on crime and immigration and began deporting first thousands, and then tens of thousands, of Central Americans each year, including many gang members.

Introduced into war-ravaged El Salvador, the gang spread quickly among demobilized soldiers and a younger generation accustomed to violence. Many deportees who had been only loosely affiliated with MS-13 in the U.S. became hard-core members after being stranded in a country they did not know, with only other gang members to rely on. As the gang proliferated and El Salvador tried to crack down on it, some deportees began finding their way back into the U.S.—in many cases bringing other, newly recruited gangsters with them. Deportation, incubation, and return: it's a cycle we've been caught in ever since.

FAST FACT

According to the US Census Bureau, 1.5 million new immigrants (legal and illegal) arrive in the United States each year.

Profiting from Deportation

Today, MS-13 has perhaps 6,000 to 10,000 members in the United States. It has grown moderately in recent years and now has a presence in 43 states (up from 32 in 2003 and 15 in 1996). Most members of the gang are foreign-born. Since 2005, ICE has arrested about 2,000 of them; 13 percent have been deported before.

Salvadoran police report that 90 percent of deported gang members return to the U.S. After several spins through the deportation-and-return cycle, MS-13 members now control many of the "coyote" services that bring aliens up from Central America. Deportation—a free trip south—can be quite profitable for those gang members who bring others back with them upon their return.

The surge in arrests and deportations in the past three years coincides with a serious U.S. effort to improve coordination with Central

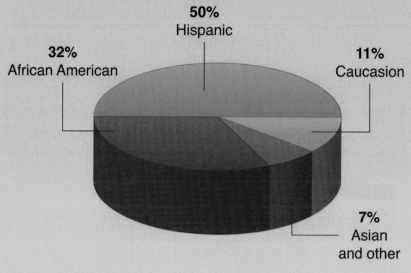

Ethnic Background of US Gang Members

50%
Hispanic

32%
African American

11%
Caucasion

7%
Asian
and other

Taken from: National Gang Center, 2010.

American governments—the better to track gang members wherever they go. But states like El Salvador have a lot to keep track of these days. MS-13 and other gangs born in the United States now have 70,000 to 100,000 members in Central America, concentrated mostly in El Salvador, Honduras, and Guatemala. The murder rate in each of these countries is now higher than that of Colombia, long the murder capital of Latin America.

Meanwhile, the U.S. continues to repeat the mistakes it made in the '90s. Most ICE arrests have been for immigration-related offenses, not criminal offenses. Suspected "associates" are lumped in with gang members, which only reinforces gang ties; with dabblers and minor offenders, experts agree that anti-gang intervention programs are better at preventing gangs' growth. For hardcore gang members, quickie deportations on immigration charges are often no more than short-term fixes; lengthy American prison sentences would be more effective.

Only the U.S. has the law-enforcement personnel, the criminal-justice system, and the money to deal with the problem. Although the idea is poison in the current political climate, the way to get rid of these gangs, paradoxically, may involve keeping them here.

EVALUATING THE AUTHOR'S ARGUMENTS:

Matthew Quirk argues that some of America's "get-tough" policies on crime and immigration—particularly the deportation of immigrant gang members—have actually led to an increase in gang violence. He suggests that imprisoning immigrant gang members in US jails would be a better way to reduce gang activity. Do you agree or disagree with Quirk? Support your answer with evidence from this volume.

Viewpoint

5

Many Youths Are Forced to Join Gangs

Kenneth Michaels, Mecca Sykes-Santana, Laurence Snyder, et al.

"Sometimes [young people] are physically threatened and forced to join gangs."

The following viewpoint is excerpted from an official report on gangs compiled by Kenneth Michaels, Mecca Sykes-Santana, Laurence Sykes, and other counselors and agents serving as staff for the State of New York Commission of Investigation. Here, the authors contend that youths are frequently coerced into joining street gangs in order to protect themselves physically and emotionally. Teenagers and children have been assaulted for refusing to join a gang, and for many "picking a side" offers safety from such attacks. Moreover, neglected children with low self-esteem often admire gangsters after seeing them glorified in the entertainment media. For these youths, gangs provide a sense of community, discipline, and respect, the authors conclude.

Kenneth Michaels, Mecca Sykes-Santana, Laurence Snyder, et al., "Introduction; Gangs' Profound Effects on Communities and Victims," *Combating Gang Activity in New York, State of New York Commission of Investigation,* May 2006, pp. 5–7, 20–22. Reproduced by permission.

AS YOU READ, CONSIDER THE FOLLOWING QUESTIONS:
1. Why might youths living in affluent areas be vulnerable to the attraction of gangs, in the authors' view?
2. What types of initiation rites do gangs often require of their members, according to the authors?
3. According to Meredith Wiley, as cited by the authors, in what ways can early childhood events make one prone to aggression and violence?

G angs are attractive to young people for a variety of reasons, and not every gang member is attracted for the same reasons. Gangs provide members with a sense of community, personal power, and a source of potential income. They provide a "family" to those whose parents fail to become involved in their lives or who simply cannot spend sufficient time with their children because they are working long hours to make ends meet.

During its [2005–2006] public hearings, the Commission [State of New York Commission of Investigation] heard testimony from Amory Sepulveda and Maureen Quintanilla, two young women whose lives were impacted by gangs. They told the Commission that some children, particularly those of immigrant parents, feel alienated from mainstream society and have a lack of self-esteem. To such youths, gangs give a sense of pride, however false. Young people are impressionable, often materialistic, and want to fit in with their peers. They are, therefore, vulnerable to the attraction of gangs even if they are financially secure. As the Commission heard, young people join gangs, even in comparatively affluent communities like Rockland County [New York] where jobs are readily available.

No Other Choice

Young people also join gangs because they believe they have no other choice. Sometimes they are physically threatened and forced to join gangs. As gangs spread, many young people feel forced to "pick a side" in order to ensure their physical safety and well-being. Noteworthy is the tragic case of sixteen-year-old Bronx student-athlete Fernando Corea, who was gunned down outside his home in February 2005, for refusing to join a street gang. Similarly, Rochester Police Officer Moses Robinson described an incident in 2004 in which an eight-year-old Brooklyn boy was "attacked and slammed to the pavement by two classmates" outside his elementary school and "ordered to choose between the Bloods and the Crips." Young people like these are vulnerable to physical and emotional attacks from gangs in their communities and in their schools. For some, the only reprieve is to pick a side.

Gang members generally must undergo some sort of initiation rite before joining a gang. Gang members may be "blessed in," which means that the member is allowed to join because his or her parent or another family member is a gang member or died as one. During one of its public hearings, the Commission heard testimony from a young woman who had been a gang member. She testified that she had been blessed into the Bloods gang because her mother was a Blood. No other steps were required for her to join the Bloods.

Brutal Initiation Rites

By contrast, other prospective gang members are "jumped in" or "beat in," a rite in which the would-be gang member is physically assaulted by current members for a prescribed period of time. Often the new member sustains very serious injuries. Former gang member Maureen Quintanilla described for the Commission how badly she was injured during her initiation rites. She also testified that, after the beating, her new comrades left her alone at a local hospital emergency room. After being treated, Ms. Quintanilla had to find her own way home.

Prospective female members are sometimes "sexed in," a ritual in which the prospective member has sexual intercourse with multiple or all male members of the gang set before being admitted. Some female gang members prefer to be "jumped in" rather than "sexed in" because of the negative stigma associated with having sex with multiple partners. Female gang members who have been "jumped in" feel that they are more respected by their male counterparts than those who were "sexed in."

Sometimes, gang members "blood in" as an initiation rite. In that ritual, prospective gang members are required to slash innocent people or commit other acts of violence. A set leader sometimes supervises the violent act to assess the would-be member's worthiness.

As Rochester Police Officer Moses Robinson noted at the Commission's October 2005 Rochester public hearing, "when we start talking about what is a gang, we have to understand . . . that if you're going to be involved in the gang, you're going to be asked to commit some criminal activity. It's not just something that you're going to join to have fun." In the month prior to the Rochester hearing, there were nine gang-related homicides in that city. The dead included three teenagers. . . .

The Ground in Which Gangs Grow

Several participants at the Commission's hearings testified about the phenomenon of ever-younger children joining gangs. While some members are born or "blessed" in, children whose families do not belong to gangs are also joining, primarily due to issues of low self-esteem. Children face a constant barrage of advertisements, music videos, and other media that glorify the gang lifestyle. These children, who have few or no role models other than sports figures and entertainers, idolize gang members and their possessions.

Often, the negative environment in which children grow up—and in which their families are forced to cope—provides fertile ground for gangs to grow. At the Commission's Rochester hearing, Rochester Institute of Technology Professor John Klofas cited an example from his research of a family's disintegration as a result of gangs. He told of a woman in northeast Rochester who had been paying her mortgage of approximately three hundred twenty-five dollars per month for fifteen years, noting that,

> as she has done that, she has watched the house across the street from her burn down, be taken down. The house next to her where there was a murder, burned down and would be taken down. The house from the other side of her, become a drug

FAST FACT

According to criminologist Terrance J. Taylor, between 30 and 60 percent of surveyed gang youths report that they joined their gangs for protection against violent assault.

house and finally be taken down. And she watched as her child grew up, and she tried to protect her child in every way . . . and have one son murdered and another son . . . go to prison for major felonies.

The Commission learned that environment does not affect children only after they begin walking and talking and interacting with people. Rather, children may become "monsters" due to events occurring in early childhood. As Meredith Wiley of Fight Crime: Invest in Kids noted,

> There is a growing body of research that shows that infancy and early childhood is a crucial developmental stage, when we form the core of conscience [and] the ability to trust . . . others. This is the time that we lay down the foundation for life-long learning and complex thinking. . . . Those kids that we have been talking about—those angry rage-filled, hate-filled kids, coming out at age 10, 12, 13, 14, didn't just wake up one morning to be that way. There was a developmental process that produced those kids that have them showing up that way. . . . Abuse and neglect [in early childhood has] a huge impact on the architecture in the neurochemistry of our brains, and they can create children who are primed for later aggression and violence.

Ms. Wiley also noted that children who are neglected or abused often continue the vicious cycle with their children.

The Effects of Stress and Neglect

Recent research allows neuroscientists to study brain growth in children. These studies have shown that stress among neglected children causes their brains to grow less and to be configured differently. Cerebral cortex abnormalities are particularly problematic because they lower the likelihood that a person will be able to control violent responses when stressed or when a person has a "primitive urge to shoot someone." While these issues are not limited to gang crime, it is clear that they have a strong connection.

Similarly, many children enter kindergarten or even first grade unprepared to learn. This lack of preparation results in frustration,

Gang members often physically intimidate children and teens to force them to join. For many, joining a gang offers safety from attacks.

and lack of interest. Many at-risk children do not have access to quality pre-kindergarten programs that prepare them for school. They begin falling behind children who are not at risk. During its investigation, the Commission learned of studies reflecting findings that at-risk children without quality pre-K programs were significantly more likely to commit violent crimes.

Once they are older, many at-risk youth feel they have little choice but to join a gang and have little perspective on the dangers of joining. A number of witnesses at the Commission's hearings commented that gangs take the place of families, which are absent in many children's lives. Children are looking for protection, a body of rules, and a sense of respect, and those needs are now being met, albeit improperly, by the street gangs. Some youths claim to be fatalists, asserting that it does not matter to them if they die or are imprisoned.

EVALUATING THE AUTHOR'S ARGUMENTS:

The authors of this viewpoint are legal counselors and agents serving on the New York State Commission of Investigation, a law enforcement agency that conducts investigations on organized crime, fraud, racketeering, and other problems of statewide importance. How does your awareness of their professional background affect your assessment of their arguments? Explain.

A Number of Risk Factors Lead Youths to Join Gangs

James C. Howell

"Multiple personal and environmental factors influence [the] choice [to join a gang]."

Young people join gangs for a multitude of reasons, explains James C. Howell in the following viewpoint. Contrary to popular opinion, youths are not usually forced into a gang; but the desire for protection, enjoyment, respect, money, or friendship may attract them to gangs, Howell contends. Youths are at a higher risk of joining a gang if they are aggressive, engage in delinquent behaviors, experience abuse or neglect, and live in communities where they feel unsafe and where many other youths are in trouble. Howell is a senior research associate with the National Gang Center in Tallahassee, Florida.

AS YOU READ, CONSIDER THE FOLLOWING QUESTIONS:
1. What are "starter gangs," according to the author?
2. According to Howell, at what age do young people typically join gangs?
3. In what way does popular culture influence at-risk youths' opinion of gangs, according to Walter B. Miller, as quoted by the author?

James C. Howell, "Gang Prevention: An Overview of Research and Programs," *Juvenile Justice Bulletin*, December 2010, pp. 3–8. Reproduced by permission.

This [viewpoint] examines how youth move from delinquency to joining gangs and how gangs form. Youth make a conscious choice to join a gang during adolescence, and multiple personal and environmental factors influence this choice.

Starter Gangs

During adolescence, peer groups and social networks form, each of which can positively or negatively influence a youth's life. Rather than immediately joining serious, violent gangs, some youth become involved in less delinquent groups, called "starter gangs."

Children and adolescents form starter gangs to introduce themselves to gang culture (i.e., distinctive attitudes, jargon, rituals, and symbols). In some areas, established gangs sometimes create cliques or sets composed of younger youth called "wannabes," "juniors," "pee wees," and the like. Where members of starter gangs may engage in minor delinquent behaviors, gang members may be involved in serious and violent offenses.

Researchers sometimes find it difficult to distinguish "gangs in embryo" from ordinary small groups of delinquents. A complicating factor is that very young gangs are extremely unstable. Adolescence is a time of changing peer relations and fleeting allegiances to both friends and gangs.

Shifting membership and an intermittent existence characterize many gangs, especially those with younger members. Because involvement in a variety of peer groups is common during adolescence, in many situations, gangs should be viewed as social networks rather than as bounded "organizations." Youth drift in and out of these groups, and even members may be unable to name all current members. In a recent survey of middle school students in nine cities, 25 percent of all gangs the students identified had been in existence for less than 1 year, and only 10 percent were said to have existed for 11 years or more.

Gang Formation

The dynamics of gang formation are complex, and researchers and practitioners have studied them from psychological, sociological, and criminological perspectives. A very popular assumption is that they grow out of conflicts among groups of young adolescents and conflicts with the law-abiding community. Where gangs are not established, they may form under extreme community conditions—particularly when youth are alienated from key socializing institutions, especially families and schools. . . .

When gangs are already established, researchers observe that the gang-joining process is similar to the manner in which most people would go about joining an organization. A youth typically begins hanging out with gang members at age 12 or 13 (even younger in some instances) and joins the gang between ages 13 and 15. This process typically takes 6 months to a year or two from the time of initial association.

FAST FACT

In the 1970s nineteen states reported youth gang problems. By the end of the twentieth century, all fifty states and the District of Columbia were reporting gang activity.

In many large cities around the United States, serious gangs have been established for years. In these circumstances, one might anticipate and yet find it difficult to prevent a youth from joining a gang. For instance, the Chicano gangs in the southwestern United States that formed in the early 1900s were populated by second-generation, "marginalized" children of extremely poor, immigrant Mexican American families who found it difficult to adjust socially and culturally to the American way of life. Youth naturally joined the gangs affiliated with their barrios (i.e., neighborhoods). After more than a half-century of continuous presence in some barrios, the Chicano gangs of Los Angeles have become institutionalized.

Attractions to Gangs

Factors that contribute to a youth's decision to join a gang fall into two categories: attractions and risk factors. This section discusses attractions to gangs.

A common public perception is that most youth are coerced into joining a gang. Quite to the contrary, most youth who join want to belong to a gang. Gangs are often at the center of appealing social actions—parties, hanging out, music, drugs, and opportunities to socialize with members of the opposite sex. The gang may be appealing because it meets a youth's social needs.

Youth reported the following reasons for joining a gang, in the order of descending importance:

- For protection.
- For fun.
- For respect.
- For money.
- Because a friend was in the gang.

These are the typical gang attractions that youth acknowledge. Of these reasons, youth most commonly join gangs for the safety they believe the gang provides. Another important influence is family members (especially siblings or cousins) who already are part of the gang, especially for Mexican American youth. Youth also occasionally cite economic reasons, such as selling drugs or making money, for joining a gang. . . .

Popular Culture

Apart from personal reasons for joining a gang, media presentations make gangs seem very appealing. The "hip" lifestyle and sensational portrayals of gangs and their members have a significant influence, particularly on more susceptible youth, for reasons that Walter B. Miller aptly explains:

In the 1950's, the musical drama *West Side Story* portrayed gang life as seen through the eyes of adult middle-class writers and presented themes of honor, romantic love, and mild rebellion consistent with the values and perspectives of these writers. In the 1990's, the substance of gang life was communicated to national audiences through a new medium known as gangsta rap. For the first time, this lifestyle was portrayed by youthful insiders, not adult outsiders. The character and values of gang life described by the rappers differed radically from the images of *West Side Story*. Language was rough and insistently obscene; women were prostitutes ("bitches," "ho's," and "sluts") to be used, beaten, and thrown away; and extreme violence and cruelty, the gang lifestyle, and craziness or insanity were glorified. Among the rappers' targets of hatred, scorn, and murder threats were police, especially black police (referred to as "house slaves" and "field hands"); other races and ethnic groups; society as a whole; and members of rival gangs. . . . Gangsta rap strengthened the desire of youth to become part of a gang subculture that was portrayed by the rappers as a glamorous and rewarding lifestyle.

Increased media popularization of gang culture has led to the point that now, [according to researcher M.W. Klein] "most young people in America recognize the look, the walk, and the talk of gang members. Many mimic it in part or in whole. Many try it out as a personal style. Play groups, break-dancing groups, taggers (i.e., graffiti artists), and school peer groups experiment with gang life." The diffusion of street gang culture in modern-day movies, music, and clothing merchandizing has served to intertwine gang culture with the general youth subculture. . . .

Friendships and Romantic Relationships

Many female adolescents are attracted to gangs because their friends or boyfriends have joined. One book looked at girls in San Antonio, TX, who hung out with male gang members. Although they were not recognized as gang members, these girls were "distinctly integrated" into the male gangs. They began hanging out with the gang in childhood, just before age 12, and at the time of the study, 40 percent reported having a boyfriend in a gang and 80 percent said they had a good friend in a male gang. Gang associations led to the girls' involvement in delinquent and criminal activities, including holding drugs (55 percent), selling drugs (31 percent), and holding weapons (27 percent). Hence, program development and service delivery should not ignore gang associates. . . .

Individual Risk Factors

A number of personal risk factors make children more likely to join gangs.

Antisocial behavior. Children whose antisocial behavior consistently worsens are most likely to join gangs. These behaviors include early involvement in delinquency, aggression, violence (without a weapon),

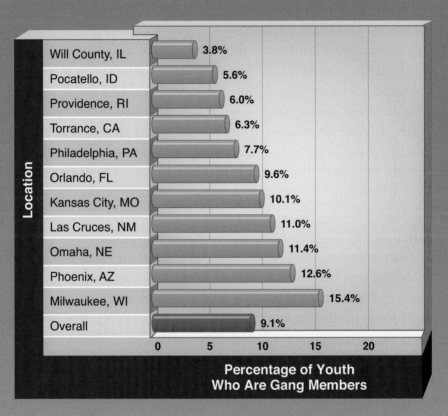

Youth Gang Membership in Selected Cities

Location	Percentage of Youth Who Are Gang Members
Will County, IL	3.8%
Pocatello, ID	5.6%
Providence, RI	6.0%
Torrance, CA	6.3%
Philadelphia, PA	7.7%
Orlando, FL	9.6%
Kansas City, MO	10.1%
Las Cruces, NM	11.0%
Omaha, NE	11.4%
Phoenix, AZ	12.6%
Milwaukee, WI	15.4%
Overall	9.1%

Taken from: James C. Howell, "Gang Prevention: An Overview of Research and Programs," *Juvenile Justice Bulletin*, December 2010.

alcohol or drug use, early dating, and precocious sexual activity. In adolescence, other forms of violence emerge—such as attacking someone with a weapon—that may also predict joining a gang.

Alcohol and drug use. Alcohol and drug use also predict joining a gang. These two early problem behaviors increase the likelihood of later gang involvement, particularly when alcohol or drug use is extensive and involves marijuana.

Mental health problems. Although little research has been done on the subject, evidence suggests that certain mental health problems in young people increase their risk of joining a gang. These problems include conduct disorders, externalizing behaviors, hyperactivity, and depression. [M.S.] Davis and [A.J.] Flannery noted that gang members in juvenile corrections facilities "often are admitted with histories of physical and sexual abuse, substance abuse, psychiatric disturbances, post-traumatic stress disorder, cognitive deficits, poor self-esteem, and other problems."

Victimization. Children who are victims of abuse or neglect are more likely to join gangs. Forms of violent victimization outside the home, such as assaults, also increase youth's risk of joining a gang.

Negative life events. Youth—particularly boys—who experience negative life events also are more likely to join gangs. These events include failing a course at school, being suspended from school, breaking up with a boyfriend/girlfriend, having a fight or problem with a friend, and the death of someone close. . . .

Community Risk Factors

As children grow older and venture out from their families, community conditions become a greater influence. Gangs tend to cluster in high-crime and economically disadvantaged neighborhoods. When gangs cluster in these neighborhoods, a number of negative conditions may arise, including:

- A greater level of criminal activity.
- A large number of neighborhood youth involved in illegal behaviors.
- Widespread availability and use of firearms and drugs.
- A small level of neighborhood attachment (i.e., positive feelings of belonging and being valued).

Unfortunately, in most distressed neighborhoods, schools, churches, and other community agencies and institutions do not provide adequate gang prevention and intervention services. . . .

A Cumulative Effect

Children who are on a trajectory of worsening antisocial behavior, including child delinquency, are more likely to join gangs during adolescence. Gang members tend to have more risk factors than other serious and violent offenders, and these factors can often be placed in multiple developmental domains. In essence, one can think of gang entry as the next developmental step in escalating delinquent behavior. Gang membership is not a product of several specific risk factors, but the result of the accumulation of many varied kinds of risk factors.

Risk factors in each of . . . five developmental domains operate collectively to increase youth's propensity to join gangs. Youth who initiate delinquent behaviors and exhibit aggression or violence at an early age (individual); experience multiple caretaker transitions (family); have numerous school-related problems (school); associate with other aggressive, gang-involved delinquents (peers); and live in communities where they feel unsafe and where many youth are in trouble (community) are at a higher risk of joining a gang.

EVALUATING THE AUTHOR'S ARGUMENTS:

James C. Howell discusses numerous reasons and risk factors that affect a youth's decision to join a gang. Compare his assertions with the assertions made by the authors of the preceding viewpoint. On what points do they agree? On what points do they disagree?

Chapter 3

How Can Gang Violence Be Reduced?

Pallbearers carry the casket of a 4-year-old boy shot and killed during a gang confrontation in the gang-plagued Echo Park neighborhood of Los Angeles.

Imprisoning Gang Members Reduces Gang Violence

Palm Beach Post

"Send the gang member to prison for a long time."

Anyone who promotes an illegal organization by committing petty crimes or by using threats to intimidate victims can be imprisoned under the Racketeer Influenced and Corrupt Organizations (RICO) Act. In the following viewpoint the editorial board of the daily *Palm Beach Post* newspaper in Florida, expresses its support for RICO laws. A gang's bad reputation is intended to instill fear in people; under RICO, gang members receive long prison sentences when prosecutors can prove that they committed crimes to boost their gang's "street rep." Imprisoning gang members gets them off the streets and reduces gang violence, the author concludes.

AS YOU READ, CONSIDER THE FOLLOWING QUESTIONS:
1. What are some of the dozens of charges against the MLK gang, according to the author?
2. How long are the sentences that two Boca Raton gang members received after being convicted of racketeering, as cited in the viewpoint?
3. How much of a decrease in gang-related homicides has Palm Beach County seen since 2006, according to Mike Wallace in the following viewpoint?

Chappy, Puchie, Whiteboy, Munchy, Piglet and Headbuster are off the streets. They were gang members who robbed, assaulted and burglarized to build their reputation and spread fear, according to the charges against them. The very deeds that gave them power are being used to take that power away.

An Effective Statute

The six men, and six more alleged members of the Lake Worth–based Making Life Krazy, or MLK, gang are in jail on charges like the ones that helped put away organized crime figures in the 1950s. The Palm Beach County Sheriff's Violent Crimes Task Force, working with State Attorney Michael McAuliffe, is successfully pursuing and breaking up gangs not with piecemeal street-corner drug arrests but with comprehensive conspiracy charges under the state [Racketeer] Influenced and Corrupt Organizations, or RICO, statute.

FAST FACT

Racketeering is the operation of an illegal business by a group.

Under that approach, thugs who are robbing people may slip beneath the radar or spend a short time in jail. But if a gang-affiliated thug robs someone, authorities can build a case that could send the gang member to prison for a long time.

The most serious of 54 charges in the MLK indictment is attempted murder in the shooting of a 13-year-old girl. Most of the charges are relatively minor: resisting arrest, criminal mischief, battery, petty theft, burglary. To make a RICO case, prosecutors must show that every act is aimed at that intangible factor known as "street rep." Gangs want a bad reputation to instill fear among victims. That's how gangs work, and that's how authorities can stop them.

RICO Is Working

It's working. Last year [2008] the sheriff's office, in coordination with the statewide prosecutor, arrested the leaders of two major Palm Beach County [Florida] gangs: Top 6 in the Boynton Beach/Lake

Worth area and Sur 13 in Westgate near Palm Beach International Airport. In January [2009], two Top 6 gang members were sentenced to 25 years for racketeering.

Recently, after a months-long undercover investigation, Boca Raton [Florida] police and the state attorney's office broke the Yung Thug Government gang of drug dealers in Boca Raton's Pearl City. Four Hondurans arrested in November [2009] face RICO charges in armed holdups of jewelry and convenience stores. Mr. McAuliffe

Law enforcement has started using the Racketeer Influenced and Corrupt Organizations (RICO) laws to arrest gang members and give them long prison sentences.

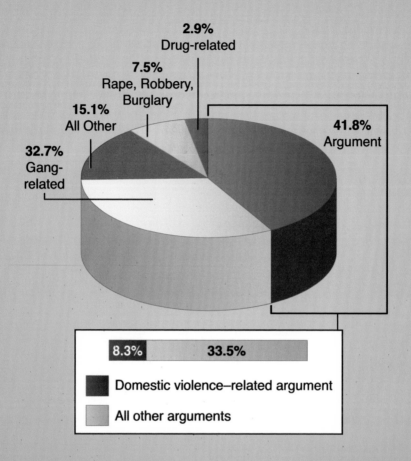

California Homicides and Contributing Circumstances

2.9%
Drug-related

7.5%
Rape, Robbery, Burglary

15.1%
All Other

32.7%
Gang-related

41.8%
Argument

8.3%   **33.5%**

Domestic violence–related argument

All other arguments

Taken from: California Department of Justice, Division of California Justice Information Services, Bureau of Criminal Information and Analysis, Criminal Justice Statistics Center. "Homicide in California 2007," p. 21. http://ag.ca.gov/cjsc /publications/homicide/hm07/preface.pdf.

has assigned a full-time prosecutor to work with the Violent Crimes Task Force. MLK is among the first successes.

Gang-related homicides countywide have fallen by nearly 50 percent since they spiked at 48 in 2006, said Lt. Mike Wallace, who leads the task force. The task force is far from done. The Yung Thugs bragged on MySpace. Other gangs remain similarly brazen. Notoriety is critical to spreading fear. Now, it's critical to ending it.

EVALUATING THE AUTHOR'S ARGUMENTS:

How would you describe the tone of this viewpoint? In your opinion, does this tone enhance the newspaper editors' main point, or detract from it? Explain your answer.

Viewpoint 2

Imprisonment Is Not the Best Way to Reduce Gang Violence

Claudia D'Allegri, Nina Martinez, Eva Valdivia, and Alexia Inigues

"We must consider solutions that support youth and families to break the cycle of violence with an alternative to incarceration."

The authors of the following viewpoint are members of the Latino Civic Alliance, a nonpartisan organization in the state of Washington that encourages Latinos to participate in civic engagement. Here, they express disagreement with a proposed state law that would focus on incarcerating gang members and impose civil injunctions that would label and limit youths' future. It lacks sufficient funding for intervention and prevention programs. Neither low-income juvenile offenders nor their families and neighborhoods ultimately benefit from such a law, these authors argue. They contend that more funding should be invested in education, job training programs that support ecomonic opportunities for youths to contribute to society, substance abuse services, gang prevention programs, and other alternatives to incarceration.

G ang violence affects communities throughout Washington state and is a legitimate concern in the lives of the families that have lost their children and loved ones.

According to the Washington State Sentencing Guidelines Commission in 2010, King County (Seattle) led in crimes committed by juveniles at 1,492 followed by Pierce County, 1,172; Clark County, 983; Yakima County, 747; Thurston County, 717; and Snohomish County, 707. However, the actual percentage of these crimes that related to gang violence is unknown. This anti-gang legislation HB 1126 unfortunately misses the mark.

Counselors talk to gang prisoners at the Washington State Penitentiary. It has been reported that out of the 10,282 juveniles detained in facilities only 1 percent have actually been convicted.

School District	Per 100 Students				
	# of 9th graders who drop out before 10th grade	# of 10th graders who drop out before 11th grade	# of 11th graders who drop out before 12th grade	# of students who drop out in 12th grade	# of students who graduate
Detroit City, MI	48	17	9	1	25
Yakima, WA	25	17	16	4	38
Los Angeles, CA	25	16	14	0	45
New York City, NY	22	29	4	0	45
Atlanta, GA	18	12	10	14	46
Kansas City, MO	26	21	7	0	46
Buffalo City, NY	24	13	7	8	48
Jefferson Parish, LA	14	14	11	7	54
Boston City, MA	21	10	1	11	57
AVERAGE	23	15	8	7	47

Taken from: Rhonda Tsoi-A-Fatt. *A Collective Responsibility, A Collective Work*. Center for Law and Social Policy, May 2008.

Stakeholders were initially led to believe that HB 1126 would invest $10 million per year in prevention programs; however in the current version, it has been reduced to $1 million. Without a comprehensive assessment, this bill leads us to believe that incarceration and injunctions are the only alternative. Funding that should have been appropriately allocated to prevention was deemed inconsequential and unnecessary.

The Need for Alternatives to Incarceration

According to a report issued by the Washington State Institute for Public Policy, alternative models to detention were found to be more effective in reducing youth offenses; $1 million will not fund successful programs. Currently, youth provider agencies that are willing to provide evidence-based treatment services lack funding to provide appropriate training for their staff.

The 2010 Washington State Sentencing Guidelines Commission report also disclosed that approximately 10,282 juveniles were held in justice facilities and only 1% were actually convicted. Among juvenile dispositions 96.4 % (9,911) were nonviolent crimes. Many of these youth are eligible for diversion treatment as an alternative to incarceration, but the scarcity of services for low-income youth is affecting their ability to receive treatment. We must consider solutions that support youth and families to break the cycle of violence with an alternative to incarceration.

This bill will increase the number of incarcerated youth without providing alternatives for diversion treatment amongst our ethnic communities. When treatment is available, many youth with gang associations desire to change their lives, but the lack of the appropriate support at the community level impacts their ability to stay clean and sober. Currently, there aren't many alternatives or job opportunities for youth after incarceration.

Investing in Programs for Our Youth

We understand that with our state facing serious budgetary constraints, it is an opportune time for legislators to consider ways to reduce juvenile justice spending that will not compromise public safety.

Rather than spending our tax dollars on incarcerating and alienating our youth we should invest in education, job training, youth and family-oriented programs, and mental health and substance abuse services.

FAST FACT

Eighty percent of those in gangs say they wish they could get out, reports the National Gang Crime Research Center.

Investments in programs and services like these can reduce the criminal justice system involvement, improve community well-being, increase the graduation rate, which is currently about 50 percent for ethnic minorities, and save money in the long run. Poor academic achievement is one of the contributing factors that hinder our Latino youth's possibilities for a prosperous future.

In our collaborative efforts with agencies and the Latino community, which is the largest ethnic minority in the state of Washington, the Latino Civic Alliance believes that HB 1126 is a path to limiting our youth's potential in becoming productive citizens in our communities. The families, communities and law enforcement officers dealing with gang violence remain foremost a priority of concern.

Furthermore, stakeholders should have accurate information and opportunity to support legislation that creates effective change and meets the needs of our communities. We are invested to support our families and respective law enforcement dealing with gang violence, and believe proactive collaborative solutions will address the root of the problem and create a successful future for our youth and our communities.

EVALUATING THE AUTHOR'S ARGUMENTS:

The authors of this viewpoint discuss a proposed state law that would invest $1 million a year in gang prevention programs. What are their objections to this proposed law? Do you think that their concerns are justified? Use evidence from the text in explaining your answer.

Children Should Participate in Antigang Programs

Katie S. Wang

"Gang members try to recruit youngsters with their flashy cars or lifestyle."

Since children are being recruited into gangs at younger ages, many experts believe that grade-school students should be involved in antigang education programs, reports Katie S. Wang in the following viewpoint. Youngsters, especially those who are poor or who live in gang-populated areas, are more easily drawn into gangs and need to learn what their options are, Wang notes. Antigang lessons may touch on issues such as neighborhood awareness or emotional skills. Wang writes for the *New Jersey Star-Ledger* and other Newark news sources.

AS YOU READ, CONSIDER THE FOLLOWING QUESTIONS:
1. What grade levels are participating in the federally funded Gang Resistance Education and Training program, according to Wang?
2. Why was social worker Mary Burke worried about the sixth graders at St. Lima School as reported in the viewpoint?
3. What did ten-year-old Ayanna Fate learn about managing her anger according to the author?

Katie S. Wang, "Anti-Gang Education for Third and Fourth Graders," *New Jersey Star-Ledger,* May 22, 2008. Reproduced by permission.

I n a second floor classroom at St. Lima School in Newark [New Jersey] today [May 22, 2008], 22 pupils were mulling over questions about anger.

What, they were asked, do they do if they are angry?

What makes them angry?

And what can they do to control their anger?

"Go to anger management class," suggested Sean Smart, a fourth-grader.

The real lesson, though, was about a topic that was never mentioned in class yesterday: gangs.

Gang Resistance Education and Training

With street gangs recruiting at a younger age, law enforcement officials are trying to get to them sooner through the federally-funded

US attorney general Eric Holder (seated, in blue) meets with community youth and families participating in the Los Angeles antigang program Summer Night Lights. Holder announced that he received five hundred thousand dollars in Recovery Act funds to support local antigang programs.

Gang Resistance Education and Training program. The state parole board's gang unit began working with sixth graders two years ago, but then expanded it to third and fourth-graders this year [2008].

"A lot of the gang members start recruiting the kids very young," said Ray Vonberheide, a senior parole officer who has worked in the street gang unit for 11 years.

Vonberheide, 40, said he has witnessed gang members try to recruit youngsters with their flashy cars or lifestyle.

"They target kids who are poor, who view these gang members as successes," said Vonberheide. "Gang members take advantage of their naivete."

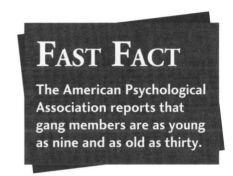

FAST FACT

The American Psychological Association reports that gang members are as young as nine and as old as thirty.

Susceptible Children

Mary Burke, a social worker with Catholic Charities in Newark, contacted Vonberheide after tensions erupted among sixth-graders at the school. At the time, she was worried the problems would escalate beyond fighting and they would hook up with gangs.

"They live in an area where they're very susceptible," she said.

Candida Esposito, an educator for more than 50 years who is now the director of staff development for the school, said the program is important because it gives children options. Even though the word, "gang" is hardly used, she said the pupils still absorb the point of the lessons.

"The more education we give them, the better," Esposito said.

St. Lima takes 220 students from Irvington and Newark, areas that are rife with gang violence.

Growing Up Fast

Vonberheide and two other officers, Hector Reyes and Dan Riccardo, have visited the school weekly, instilling a different lesson each time. A few weeks ago, they broached the topic of gangs more candidly by asking the pupils if they've heard of or seen gang members lurking in their neighborhoods.

"I've started to notice how much younger our criminals seem to look!"

"I've started to notice how much younger our criminals seem to look," cartoon by Ray Jelliffe. www.Cartoon Stock.com. Copyright © by Ray Jelliffe. Reproduction rights obtainable from www.CartoonStock.com.

A lot of the students, Vonberheide said, were very aware that gangs are present on the streets.

"They're growing up too fast," he said. "These are things kids shouldn't know about."

Today's primary lesson was to pause and think twice when they get angry.

Ayanna Fate, 10, said when other kids call her names and tease her, she reacts by hitting objects around her. After yesterday's lesson, she said she plans to respond differently in the future.

"I'm going to drink water," she said. "It soothes your mind."

EVALUATING THE AUTHOR'S ARGUMENTS:

Katie S. Wang explains that Gang Resistance Education and Training programs are now being offered to children as young as eight years of age. Considering what you know on the topic, is this a good age to begin teaching children about gangs? Should even younger children be involved in such programs? Defend your answer with evidence from the text.

Viewpoint

4

Parents Should Monitor Their Children for Potential Gang Activity

"It's a good thing for parents to be aware of what their child is doing in school, on the Internet and in their spare time."

Monica Springer

In the following viewpoint Monica Springer outlines several gang-awareness pointers that law enforcement experts believe all parents need to learn. Because gangs often recruit young children, these experts contend that parents should know what their children are doing at all times. Police encourage parents to keep a watchful eye on their children's friendships, online behaviors, school functions, notebooks, and bedrooms; moreover, a zero-tolerance policy against drugs, alcohol, and gang activity should be maintained. Springer is a newspaper reporter at the *Emporia Gazette* in Emporia, Kansas.

AS YOU READ, CONSIDER THE FOLLOWING QUESTIONS:

1. What advice does Kelly Rodriguez offer to parents who do not speak English, according to the author?
2. What are some of the warning signs that a child is engaging in gang activity, according to police and as cited by the author?
3. What can parents do if they suspect their child is involved in gang activity, as reported in the viewpoint?

It starts early and it starts at home, members of law enforcement said at a gang awareness meeting Thursday night [April 23, 2009] at Kenneth Henderson Middle School. Members of the Garden City [Kansas] Police Department, Finney County Sheriff's Office, along with Youth Services, were on hand to point out signs that a child might be in a gang and what to do to prevent a child from being involved in gang activity. Kelly Rodriguez, gang resource officer for Youth Services, and Sgt. Steve Martinez with the sheriff's office stressed the importance

FAST FACT

The National Parent Teacher Association contends that children should be taught very early—from age four or five—that gangs are dangerous and do not provide positive support.

Law enforcement officials urge parents to monitor their children's online activities and their social networking sites, such as MySpace and Facebook, for potential gang-related activity.

Risk Factors for Juvenile Crime

Domain	Risk Factor		Protective Factor*
	Early Onset (age 6–11)	Late Onset (age 12–14)	
Individual	• General offenses • Substance use • Being male • Aggression** • Psychological condition • Hyperactivity • Problem (antisocial) behavior • Exposure to television violence • Medical, physical problems • Low IQ • Antisocial attitudes, beliefs • Dishonesty**	• General offenses • Psychological condition • Restlessness • Difficulty concentrating** • Risk taking • Aggression** • Being male • Physical violence • Antisocial attitudes, beliefs • Crimes against persons • Problem (antisocial) behavior • Low IQ • Substance use	• Intolerant attitude toward deviance • High IQ • Being female • Positive social orientation • Perceived sanctions for transgressions
Family	• Low socioeconomic status/poverty • Antisocial parents • Poor parent-child relations • Harsh, lax, or inconsistent discipline • Broken home • Separation from parents • Other conditions • Abusive parents • Neglect	• Poor parent-child relationship • Harsh, lax discipline; poor monitoring, supervision • Low parental involvement • Antisocial parents • Broken home • Low socioeconomic status/poverty • Abusive parents • Other conditions • Family conflict**	• Warm, supportive relationships with parents or other adults • Parents' positive evaluation of peers • Parental monitoring
School	• Poor attitude, performance	• Poor attitude, performance • Academic failure	• Commitment to school • Recognition for involvement in conventional activities
Peer Group	• Weak social ties • Antisocial peers	• Weak social ties • Antisocial, delinquent peers • Gang membership	• Friends who engage in conventional behavior
Community		• Neighborhood crime, drugs • Neighborhood disorganization	

*Age of onset not known   **Males only

Taken from: *Youth Violence: A Report of the Surgeon General*, 2001.

of parents being involved in their children's lives. Gangs often recruit children at young ages, and it's best to know the warning signs, she said. For example, they said, it's a good thing for parents to be aware of what their child is doing in school, on the Internet and in their spare time. Rodriguez and Martinez cautioned parents to examine their children's online social networking Web sites, put the family computer in a public place in the home and to not allow locks on children's bedroom doors.

Watch for Possible Signs of Gang Activity

Rodriguez said many parents who don't speak English rely on their children to communicate when they go out in public. He said that doesn't mean the children can dictate rules in a household. "It's your house. Look in their notebooks. Look in their bedrooms," Rodriguez said. Law enforcement also encourages parents to monitor their children's online activity, including the social networking Web site MySpace. Rodriguez said it's essential for parents to look on their child's MySpace page, and urged them to look at their profile, not their homepage. "It's really important for parents to monitor activities on the computer. If their kid's page is private, ask to look at it," Martinez said. Rodriguez and Martinez, along with several police officers, offered some warning signs to parents. Signs of gang activity include: If your child suddenly wants privacy; has unexplained cash, CDs, clothes or jewelry; has unexplained bruises or other physical injuries; a change in good grades; lies about activities; doesn't let parents meet their friends; starts using drugs or alcohol or becomes obsessed with one color or brand of clothing. Tips law enforcement offers parents include: be good listeners; keep kids busy in activities; know where and what your children are doing; establish no tolerance rules when it comes to gang activity, drugs and alcohol; and don't be afraid to search a child's room or ask that a school searches a child's locker. This is the fourth meeting law enforcement officials have conducted about gang awareness in Garden City schools. The meetings have been sparsely attended, which makes it more difficult to tell parents what to look for, police officers and sheriff's deputies said.

If a parent thinks their child may be involved in gang activity, or if a parent is concerned about their child, they can request that a law enforcement official speak to the child.

EVALUATING THE AUTHOR'S ARGUMENTS:

This selection presents suggestions from law enforcement officials on what parents should be doing to keep their children away from gangs. Do you agree that concerned parents should feel free to scan their children's online activities and search their notebooks and bedrooms? Or could such actions be counterproductive? Explain.

Viewpoint

5

The Scared Straight Program Reduces Criminal Activity Among Youths

Nick Lehr

"[After Scared Straight], shell-shocked teens vow to avoid prison at all costs."

The 1978 documentary *Scared Straight* follows a group of teen delinquents as they visit a prison where they are confronted and verbally abused by inmates. This experience, intended to shock the youths out of committing crimes that could lead to their own incarceration, became the basis of more movies and Scared Straight delinquency-prevention programs in the ensuing decades. In this viewpoint Nick Lehr praises Scared Straight, arguing that it gives at-risk youths a foretaste of what might be ahead for them and provides them an opportunity to change their ways. Lehr, a Stanford University graduate, writes for the *Good Men Project Magazine* and blog.

1. Why does the author feel sympathy for executed criminal David Mason?
2. What is the documentary *Gladiator Days* about, according to Lehr?
3. What feedback has filmmaker Arnold Shapiro received about his documentary *Scared Straight,* as cited by the author?

Everyone knows prison is brutal. Most would rather not think about it.

The men inside casually discuss committing appalling crimes. They wallow in cold, cramped cells with their volatile, dangerous peers.

Some are young when they first committed their crimes, like Eric Smith, who at 13 lured 4-year-old Derrick Robie into the woods near his house, strangled him, and smashed in his face with rocks.

More often than not, they've had horrific childhoods. This is where my sympathy lies—with criminals like David Mason, who was executed in 1993 after going on a killing spree. In Mason's case, were the murders committed when he pulled the trigger? Or did they originate 15 years earlier, when he was locked in a windowless room dubbed "the dungeon" by his fundamentalist Christian parents? When he was beaten with a pancake turner, and forced to wear a soiled diaper on his head to school whenever he wet the bed? When his father would strap him to his workbench, gag him, and beat him unconscious?

Once incarcerated, everyone deals with prison life differently. Do you give up? Lash out? Or do you adapt? We can't even speculate how we'd react, because we exist within a context and possess a perspective that is so far removed from that of prison life.

Unraveling Behind Bars

Some prisoners pass the days focusing on old (or newfound) passions, using what little resources they have. They make doll houses, paint on the backs of postcards with M&Ms, write novels, or compose music.

Others unravel further behind bars.

"When I got incarcerated, I declared war on the state of Indiana," announces "predatory" inmate Darren Bailey on MSNBC's *Lockup: Raw*. "They gave me an excessive sentence as a result of my crime. Well, I'm giving you excessive violence as the result of my anger."

The HBO documentary *Gladiator Days* examines the case of Utah State Prison inmate Troy Kell. In 1994 Kell, a white supremacist who was already serving a life sentence for committing a murder at the age of 18, killed black inmate Lonnie Blackmon in plain sight of prisoners and guards.

It was all caught on tape.

In the video, Kell methodically stabs Blackmon 67 times as unarmed guards watch behind locked-down doors. Once Blackmon stops breathing, Kell, adrenaline surging, paces around the room, drying his bloodied hands with a towel. "Let's get some white power

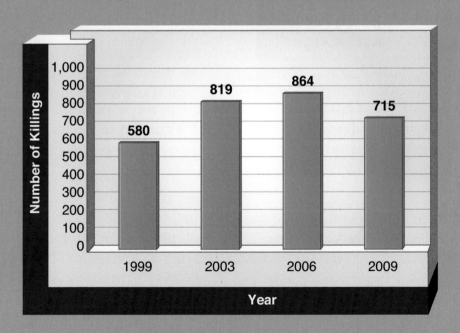

Taken from: Federal Bureau of Investigation. *Crime in the United States*, 2010.

jumpin' off in here," he barks. Fellow inmates hoot and holler from their cells. A full five minutes pass before guards dressed in riot gear bull-rush the room to subdue Kell.

His interview is chilling:

Producer: *Why did you stab him so many times?*

Kell: *All I can tell is—he kept moving. I just stabbed the shit out of him until he didn't move anymore.*

The Realities of Prison Life

Scared Straight conveys, first hand, the realities of prison life: the unpredictability, the loneliness, the monotony, and the inmates—like Troy Kell, locked up for life—who have nothing to lose. It's a dog-eat-dog world, where guards exist merely to maintain order, not to protect the lives and well-being of individual inmates.

Teens who enter adult prisons are most vulnerable. They often have no idea what they're in for, but the reality sinks in quickly—usually at the first meal—when they're harassed by hardened inmates who taunt and threaten them, or coo at the "fresh meat" before their eyes.

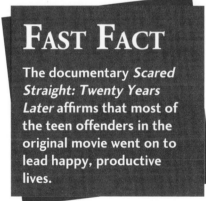

FAST FACT

The documentary *Scared Straight: Twenty Years Later* affirms that most of the teen offenders in the original movie went on to lead happy, productive lives.

This is the beauty of Arnold Shapiro's 1978 documentary *Scared Straight*: it provides at-risk teens a preview of the path they're on, a taste of the future before them, while giving them the opportunity to change their ways.

Shapiro's film documents a group of juvenile delinquents, cocky and self-assured, as they enter prison for the first time. Their confident demeanor quickly crumbles as they sit helplessly before the "lifers" who berate and verbally abuse them, while divulging snapshots of the misery they endure on a daily basis.

When we get sexual desires, who do you think we get? And don't tell me each other!

As part of a Scared Straight program, an inmate describes the hellish prison conditions a youth can expect in prison if he does not give up drugs and gangs. Many feel the program has been highly successful.

Upon leaving the prison, a number of the shell-shocked teens vow to avoid prison at all costs.

Brutally Effective

30 years later, the film, which won an Oscar for best documentary feature, is still brutally effective.

"I still get comments about *Scared Straight* from people who tell me they were juvenile offenders," Shapiro explains. "Their parents made them watch it, and it was either the single cause of their change or a major factor."

Shapiro continues to be amazed at *Scared Straight*'s success; it has since become a cultural icon, and a number of prisons have instituted similar programs.

"When I made *Scared Straight*, I had no idea it was going to become an iconic film. I had no idea I would continue to receive letters from parents and teachers and young people, year after year after year, once it was in educational distribution. It just never went away."

EVALUATING THE AUTHOR'S ARGUMENTS:

The author argues that Scared Straight programs frighten young delinquents out of their complacency, keeping them from committing crimes that would land them in prison. In light of what you have read elsewhere in this text, do you think such programs are an effective way to steer teens away from gangs? Or do you think that there are other gang-prevention strategies that would have a greater impact on young people? Explain.

The Scared Straight Program Is Ineffective

Laurie O. Robinson and Jeff Slowikowski

"These programs [do] not deter teenage participants from offending."

In the following viewpoint Laurie O. Robinson and Jeff Slowikowski argue that Scared Straight programs, modeled after a documentary of the same name, do not deter juvenile crime and may actually be harmful. Scared Straight programs allow at-risk youth to briefly experience the harsh realities of prison in an attempt to shock them into changing their behavior. According to these authors, however, such programs actually make participating teens *more* likely to commit future crimes. Mentoring programs and positive role models are much more effective at changing a youth's behavior, they explain. Robinson is an assistant attorney general for the US Office of Justice Programs. Slowikowski is acting administrator of the federal Office of Juvenile Justice and Delinquency Prevention.

AS YOU READ, CONSIDER THE FOLLOWING QUESTIONS:
  1. According to the viewpoint, what is *Beyond Scared Straight*?
  2. In what ways have Scared Straight programs proved to be harmful, according to the authors?
  3. In the authors' opinion, what are the benefits of long-term mentoring relationships for youths?

"Scared straight" programs have long been wildly popular in this country as a get-tough response to juvenile crime. They typically involve bringing at-risk youths into an adult prison, where they are confronted—in shocking and brutal fashion—by adult inmates. These programs may include tours of the facility and personal stories from prisoners and may even integrate the youths into the prison population for up to a day. Experiencing the harsh reality of life behind bars is thought to deter kids from a life of crime by frightening them into changing their behavior.

The A&E Network is currently airing "Beyond Scared Straight," a series highlighting four of these programs across the country. A recent episode followed five youths who were brought to the Maryland Correctional Institution at Jessup, which houses more than 1,000 inmates. These youths came face to face with what the A&E website described as "menacing inmates, including convicted murderers, [who] surround the kids and taunt them." The network portrays such programs as effective in keeping youths from becoming lifelong criminals.

> ## FAST FACT
>
> Angelo Speziale, featured as a youth in the original 1979 *Scared Straight* film, was later sentenced to twenty-five years in prison for rape and murder.

Scary and Ineffective

Unfortunately, the research tells us otherwise: "scared straight" is not only ineffective but is potentially harmful. And it may run counter to the law.

Anthony Petrosino and a team of researchers from the Campbell Collaboration, an international research network, analyzed the findings from evaluations of nine scared straight–type programs. In contrast to the claims of proponents, Mr. Petrosino and his colleagues found that these programs did not deter teenage participants from offending; in fact, they were *more* likely to offend in the future. Across the evaluated programs, participants were up to 28 percent more likely to offend than youths who didn't participate. To add insult to injury, a number of youths reported to evaluators that adult inmates sexually propositioned them, and tried to steal their belongings. Not only was scared straight found not to deter criminal behavior, the study strongly suggested the program caused harm.

Law enforcement officials give teen youths a tour of the Livingston County, Michigan, jail as part of a sixteen-step Moral Reconation Therapy program designed to show youth the cold realities of life in prison. Critics say it is ineffective, potentially harmful, and may run counter to the law.

Mentoring Effects on Teen Behavior

- Initiating drug use—down 45.8%
- Skipped class—down 36.7%
- Skipped day of school—down 52.2%
- Number of times hit someone—down 31.7%
- Initiating Alcohol Use—down 27.4%
- Scholastic competence—up 4.3%
- Grades—up 3%

Taken from: "An Evaluation of Big Brother/Big Sister Sites," *Juvenile Justice Bulletin*, April 1997.

The fact that these types of programs are still being touted as effective, despite stark evidence to the contrary, is troubling. In the decades following the original scared straight program, states across the country developed similar models in the hopes that this get-tough approach would make an impact on their impressionable youth. As it turns out, the impact was not the one they had hoped for.

No Funding for Scared Straight

Fortunately, in recent years, policymakers and criminal and juvenile justice practitioners have begun to recognize that answers about what works are best found in sound research, not in storytelling. Evidence from science provides the field with the best tool for sound decision-making. This "smart on crime" approach saves taxpayer money and maximizes limited government resources—especially critical at a time of budget cuts.

In light of this evidence, the U.S. Department of Justice discourages the funding of scared straight–type programs. States that operate such programs could have their federal funding reduced if shown not to have complied with the Juvenile Justice and Delinquency Prevention Act.

What Works Best?

So what does research tell us about what *does* work? Mentoring programs have been found to be effective in reducing incidents of delinquency, substance use and academic failure in participating youth. Mentoring is a process that uses positive relationships to teach, impart or institute changes in a youth's behavior or attitudes. Research has shown that mentoring relationships that last at least 12 months or through an entire school year are most effective. Further, youth in long-term mentoring relationships tend to improve their self-esteem, social skills and outlook about their future.

The Department of Justice has supported mentoring programs for more than 30 years as a primary prevention tool to address juvenile delinquency. Not surprisingly, research suggests that offering at-risk youth a relationship with a positive role model has more benefit than scaring them with a negative one.

It is understandable why desperate parents hoping to divert their troubled children from further misbehavior would place their hopes in a program they see touted as effective on TV, and why in years past policymakers opted to fund what appeared to be an easy fix for juvenile offending. However, we have a responsibility—as both policymakers and parents—to follow evidence, not anecdote, in finding answers, especially when it comes to our children.

EVALUATING THE AUTHOR'S ARGUMENTS:

The authors of this viewpoint maintain that Scared Straight programs are not effective deterrents to juvenile crime and that they may actually be harmful. What evidence do they use to support their argument? Do you find this evidence persuasive? Why or why not?

Communities, Law Enforcement, and Government Must Work Together to Reduce Gang Violence

"Only by having parents, community organizations ... governments, law enforcement agencies and school districts working together can we ... put a crimp on gang violence."

Yakima Herald-Republic

In the following viewpoint the editorial board of the *Yakima Herald-Republic* writes that civic and community leaders must make public safety their top priority if they hope to stop gang violence. Moreover, deterring gang activity will require all levels of the community—including youths, parents, teachers, police, city councils, school districts, and civic organizations—to work together responsibly, each contributing what they can toward outreach, counseling, training, security, and law enforcement. The *Yakima Herald-Republic* is a daily newspaper in Yakima, Washington.

AS YOU READ, CONSIDER THE FOLLOWING QUESTIONS:
  1. How many gang-related deaths occurred in 2008 in King County, Washington, according to the author?
  2. Why are lawmakers in central Washington hesitant to devote more funds to the battle against gangs, according to the author?
  3. What does the author say is the most important step in reducing gang violence?

A nother day, another shooting. Police in Grandview [Washington] were on the hunt Wednesday night [June 2009] for a 19-year-old man who apparently shot a rival gang member, a 14-year-old, in a drive-by shooting. The victim suffered superficial wounds. "We know who it is," the Grandview police chief said of the shooter. That can also be said of the growing gang problem. We know violence is increasing and we know many of the culprits causing it. What we can't seem to settle on is how to solve it. For years, those living on the west side of the state have pointed an accusing finger at Central Washington and the city of Yakima, in particular, as a breeding ground for gangs. That's

FAST FACT

During a single June 2010 weekend, fifty-four people were shot in Chicago, Illinois—mostly as a result of gang violence.

no longer the case. In Seattle, gang violence has hit home. Last year, King County recorded 17 gang-related deaths. At a recent Seattle City Hall forum, a U.S. District Court judge compared Seattle's gang infestation to a "pandemic"—an infectious disease that spreads easily and can kill large numbers of people.

Everyone Must Contribute

But it's also important to note what others said at the forum. That police can not "arrest their way" out of this gang problem. That parents must take more responsibility for raising their children by providing a loving home where honesty prevails and listening to each other is encouraged. That educators continue to find ways of keeping students

A mural hanging over a Philadelphia community basketball court illustrates the consequences of gang violence. In the author's opinion, only by working together can parents, law enforcement agencies, community organizations, city and state governments, and school districts hope to curb gang violence.

in school and off the streets. That communities provide activities to keep young boys and girls involved and engaged. Seattle has already approved a two-year $8 million initiative that pays for specialized services such as street outreach, counseling, mentoring, anger management, education and job training. It's focused on approximately 800 young people who are now involved in the juvenile-justice system or who have been frequently suspended from middle school for violent behavior.

One Street Corner and One Youth at a Time

Here in the Yakima Valley, million-dollar initiatives have had mixed results. Voters approved a countywide sales tax increase in 2004 that paid for increased law enforcement and court funding. Last year alone, the sales tax boost accounted for $8.3 million. Since it had a six-year sunset clause, the measure will be back on the ballot this November for renewal. In the city of Yakima, though, voters three years ago defeated a ballot measure that would have raised utility taxes to pay for additional police and prosecutors along with improved court and jail services. It would have raised $1 million annually over a four-year period. In

Olympia, lawmakers did have success last year in pushing through a sweeping bill that redefined criminal gang activity, increased sentences for adults who recruit juveniles and created a statewide gang information database that allows law enforcement agencies to track known gang members. Rep. Charles Ross, R-Naches, helped to shape that measure and tried in vain to increase new criminal justice programs during this year's session. But with a looming $9 billion revenue shortfall, lawmakers had no desire to boost spending even in the face of increased gang violence across the state. Absent new funds to aid in the battle against gangs, communities in Central Washington will have to collectively roll up their sleeves and get to work, one street corner and one youth at a time. More block watches will have to be embraced; law enforcement agencies will need to build stronger partnerships with civic organizations. City councils will also need to step forward and make public safety their No. 1 goal. Ever since the city of Yakima saw its Safe Community Action Plan defeated at the ballot box three years ago, the City Council has seemed less engaged with the issue of gang violence. That needs to change, and in a hurry. Only by having parents, community organizations, city and county governments, law enforcement agencies and school districts working together can we begin to put a crimp on gang violence. And most importantly, we need to bring young men and young women into the process. Without them, we will have failed the very people our communities are trying to reach.

EVALUATING THE AUTHOR'S ARGUMENTS:

In this viewpoint the editorial board of the *Yakima Herald-Republic* lists several suggestions on what people should do to address gang violence in a community where antigang programs are underfunded. Compare and contrast the board's argument with the authors of the first two viewpoints in this chapter. Which of these viewpoints do you think offers the most promising solution to the problem of gang violence? Use textual evidence in defending your answer.

Facts About Gangs

Editor's note: These facts can be used in reports or papers to reinforce or add credibility when making important points or claims.

Gang Membership and Gang-Related Crime

According to the 2009 US National Gang Threat Assessment:

- Up to 80 percent of crimes are gang related. Typical gang-related crimes include armed robbery, assault, auto theft, drug trafficking, extortion, fraud, identity theft, home invasions, murder, and weapons trafficking.
- Many gangs actively use the Internet to recruit new members and to communicate with members in different countries.
- One out of one hundred men between the ages of fifteen and sixty-five is a member of a gang.
- Gangs are the primary distributors of illegal drugs in the United States.
- The Midwest was the US region that experienced the greatest increase in gang population during the first decade of the twentieth century.

According to the Office of Juvenile Justice and Delinquency Prevention:

- A survey of nine thousand US adolescents found that 8 percent of youths between the ages of 12 and 17 belong or have belonged to a gang.
- Between 15 and 32 percent of youths aged 12 to 17 in high-risk areas of large cities belong or have belonged to a gang.

According to the Bureau of Justice Statistics:

- In Chicago, Illinois, gang membership was up to 105,000 in 2010 from nearly 70,000 in 2000.
- In Los Angeles, California, gang membership was up to 45,000 in 2010 from about 43,000 in 2008.

- Sixty-seven percent of killings involving young men ages twenty-five to thirty-four are gang-related.

According to the August 2010 National Survey of American Attitudes on Substance Abuse, 35 percent of middle school students and 45 percent of high school students say there are gangs or students who consider themselves to be part of a gang in their schools.

According to the Office of Security and Emergency Management:
- Gang members are sixty times more likely to be killed than non-gang members.
- About 95 percent of hard-core gang members are high-school dropouts.
- The average age of a gang member is twenty.

Facts on Gangs Worldwide
- The estimated US gang population is 1 million members of about 20,000 gangs, according to the 2009 National Gang Threat Assessment.
- According to the *New York Times*, the Pine Ridge Indian Reservation in South Dakota has 39 gangs with 5,000 members.
- National Public Radio claims that Navajo country has reported 225 gangs in its territory.
- The *Observer* reports that there are between 25,000 and 50,000 gang members in El Salvador.
- The *Sun* reports that there are more than 1,000 gangs in the United Kingdom.
- According to the *Washington Times*, the Mexican drug cartels have as many as 100,000 foot soldiers.
- Four Italian organized crime groups include 20,000 members and 250,000 affiliates worldwide, according to the Federal Bureau of Investigation.

Organizations to Contact

The editors have compiled the following list of organizations concerned with the issues debated in this book. The descriptions are derived from materials provided by the organizations. All have publications or information available for interested readers. The list was compiled on the date of publication of the present volume; the information provided here may change. Be aware that many organizations take several weeks or longer to respond to inquiries, so allow as much time as possible for the receipt of requested materials.

American Civil Liberties Union (ACLU)
125 Broad St., 18th Fl.
New York, NY 10004
(212) 549-2500
website: www.aclu.org

The ACLU is a national organization that works to defend Americans' civil rights as guaranteed by the US Constitution. It opposes sentencing juvenile criminals to life without parole and seeks to protect the public-assembly rights of gang members or people associated with gangs. The ACLU website includes an archive of key issues with links to articles on juvenile justice, including "Life Without a Chance," and "From Filthy Boys Prison to New Beginnings: Hill Staffers Walk a Mile in Youthful Offenders' Shoes."

Boys and Girls Clubs of America
1275 Peachtree St. NE
Atlanta, GA 30309-3506
(404) 487-5700
e-mail: info@bgca.org
website: www.bgca.org

Boys and Girls Clubs of America supports juvenile gang intervention programs in its individual clubs throughout the United States. For example, the organization's Delinquency and Gang Prevention

Initiative targets at-risk youth from the ages of six to eighteen, teaching them violence-prevention strategies and directing them to positive alternatives. The position paper "Our Nation's Dropout Crisis Is Everyone's Problem" is available at the Boys and Girls Clubs of America website.

Center for the Study and Prevention of Violence (CSPV)
Institute of Behavioral Science, University of Colorado at Boulder
483 UCB, Boulder, CO 80309
(303) 492-1032
fax: (303) 492-2151
e-mail: cspv@colorado.edu
website: www.colorado.edu

The CSPV was founded in 1992 to provide information and assistance to organizations that are dedicated to preventing violence, particularly youth violence. Its website includes an information clearinghouse with links to fact sheets, publications, and editorials, including "Gangs and Adolescent Violence," "What Is a Safe School?" and "Reponse to *Beyond Scared Straight* on A&E."

Child Welfare League of America (CWLA)
1726 M St. NW, Ste. 500
Washington, DC 20036
(202) 688-4200
fax: (202) 833-1689
website: www.cwla.org

Founded in 1920, the CWLA is a coalition of private and public agencies that works to improve care and services for abused, dependent, or neglected children, youth, and their families. It publishes information on gangs and youth crime in the bimonthly *Children's Voice* magazine and the scholarly journal *Child Welfare*. A News and Media Center, available at its website, provides links to articles, statements, and editorials such as "The Poverty That Budget-Cutters Can't Ignore" and "Bad Boys Bring Lessons."

John Howard Society of Canada
809 Blackburn Mews
Kingston, ON K7P 2N6 Canada
(613) 384-6272

fax: (613) 384-1847
e-mail: national@johnhoward.ca
website: www.johnhoward.ca

The John Howard Society of Canada is a nonprofit agency that aims to find effective, just, and humane responses to the causes and consequences of crime. It works with people who might or who have come into conflict with the law, offering counseling, training, and employment services to men in correctional facilities, young offenders in custody, and people at risk of becoming involved in crime. Its website provides resources for understanding crime and justice trends in Canada, including "Where Are We Going with Drug Policy and What Should We Do About It?"

National Alliance of Gang Investigators' Associations (NAGIA)
PO Box 782
Elkhorn, NE 68022
(402) 510-8581
website: www.nagia.org

Formed in 1998, NAGIA is a cooperative organization representing nineteen state and regional gang investigators associations with over twenty thousand members. It provides leadership in developing and recommending strategies to prevent and control gang crime, administers professional training, and assists criminal justice professionals and the public in tracking gangs, gang members, and gang crime around the world. Its home page provides an archive of "Gangs in the News" articles.

National Gang Center
Institute for Intergovernmental Research
PO Box 12729
Tallahassee, FL 32317
(850) 385-0600
fax: (850) 386-5356
e-mail: information@nationalgangcenter.gov
website: www.nationalgangcenter.gov

The National Gang Center website features the latest research about gangs and gang-prevention programs and provides links to tools, databases, and other resources to assist with the creation of effective community-based gang intervention and suppression strategies.

Visitors can read and download publications related to street gangs, register for antigang training courses, and look up gang-related state laws and municipal codes. Reports available in its publications archive include *Menacing or Mimicking? Realities of Youth Gangs* and *Graffiti*.

National Gang Crime Research Center (NGCRC)
PO Box 990
Peotone, IL 60468-0990
(708) 258-9111
fax: (708) 258-9546
e-mail: gangcrime@aol.com
website: www.ngcrc.com

The NGCRC is a nonprofit independent agency that conducts research on gangs and gang members and disseminates information through publications and reports. It publishes the quarterly *Journal of Gang Research* and the special report *Gang Banging on Facebook: Should We Look the Other Way?* is available at its website.

National School Safety Center (NSSC)
141 Duesenberg Dr., Ste. 7B
Westlake Village, CA 91362
(805) 373-9977
e-mail: info@schoolsafety.us
website: www.schoolsafety.us

The NSSC was established in 1984 as a joint program between the United States Departments of Education and Justice. It is now an independent nonprofit organization serving schools and communities worldwide by providing training and technical assistance in the areas of safe school planning and school crime prevention. The NSSC publishes a variety of publications and multimedia resources that support safe and welcoming schools, including *School Crime and Violence: Victims' Rights* and the newsletter *School Safety Update*.

Office of Juvenile Justice and Delinquency Prevention (OJJDP)
810 Seventh St. NW
Washington, DC 20531
(202) 307-5911
website: www.ojjdp.gov

As the primary US federal agency charged with monitoring and improving the juvenile justice system, the OJJDP supports states, local communities, and tribal jurisdictions in their efforts to develop effective anticrime and corrections programs for juveniles. Through its Juvenile Justice Clearinghouse, the OJJDP distributes fact sheets, the annual National Youth Gang Survey, and reports such as *Youth Gangs in Indian Country* and *Hybrid and Other Modern Gangs*.

Teens Against Gang Violence (TAGV)
2 Moody St.
Dorchester, MA 02124
(617) 282-9659
e-mail: teensagv@aol.com
website: www.tagv.org

TAGV is a volunteer, community-based, teen peer-leadership program. Through presentations and workshops, TAGV educates youths, parents, schools, and community groups about violence, crime, racism, weapons, drug abuse, and other issues of concern to at-risk communities. More information on its programs are available at its website.

For Further Reading

Books

Boyle, Gregory. *Tattoos on the Heart: The Power of Boundless Compassion.* New York: Free Press, 2010. The author is the founder of Homeboy Industries, an organization that provides job training and encouragement to young people in neighborhoods with a high concentration of gang activity. He maintains that commitment, sharing, and unconditional love can transform the lives of gang-involved youth.

Caine, Alex. *Befriend and Betray: Infiltrating the Hells Angels, Bandidos, and Other Criminal Brotherhoods.* New York: St. Martin's, 2009. The author chronicles his twenty-five years as an undercover agent infiltrating various organized criminal groups and gangs to bring them to justice.

Juette, Melvin, and Ronald J. Berger. *Wheelchair Warrior: Gangs, Disability, and Basketball.* Philadelphia: Temple University Press, 2009. A young gang member, paralyzed by a bullet, becomes a top wheelchair athlete.

Logan, Samuel. *This Is for the Mara Salvatrucha: Inside the MS-13, America's Most Violent Gang.* New York: Hyperion, 2009. A journalist based in Latin America tells the story of Brenda Paz, a Honduran-American teenager who belonged to the MS-13 gang. Paz becomes an informant for the FBI and exposes the dark and violent world of this often elusive and ruthless gang.

Rodriguez, Luis J. *Always Running: La Vida Loca—Gang Days in L.A.* New York: Touchstone, 2005. The author documents his youth as an East Los Angeles gang member, with hopes of steering his own teenage son away from the gang he recently joined.

Savelli, Lou. *Gangs Across America and Their Symbols.* Flushing, NY: Looseleaf, 2005. A pocket guide to various gangs' color schemes, graffiti, tattoos, hand signs, and slang.

Swift, Richard. *Gangs: A Groundwork Guide.* Toronto, ON: Groundwood, 2012. The author examines the worldwide growth of gangs in recent years, focusing on root causes such as poverty, alienation, racism, immigration policies, dysfunctional families, and the need for social bonding and identity.

Venkatesh, Sudhir. *Gang Leader for a Day: A Rogue Sociologist Takes to the Streets.* New York: Penguin, 2008. The author is a young sociologist who befriends drug dealers and embeds himself in Chicago's most notorious gang to observe the daily lives and struggles of gang members.

Periodicals and Internet Sources

Agren, David. "Self-Rule on the Rise in Mexico's Prisons," *USA Today*, April 29, 2011.

Bentham, Martin. "New Nickname or Slang? How to Spot if Your Child Is in a Gang," *Evening Standard* (London), September 2, 2008.

Buffalo News. "Targeting West-Side Gangs: FBI Crackdown with Racketeering Law a Good Part of Anti-Violence Arsenal," September 28, 2010.

Castro, Tony. "Anti-Gang Groups Face New Scrutiny," *Daily News of Los Angeles*, August 11, 2009.

Clurfeld, Andrea. "'Scarface' vs. Shakespeare: Amid Violence, Peer Pressure, Kids Face Choices in School," *Asbury Park (NJ) Press* April 2, 2010.

Conery, Ben. "Justice's Anti-Gang Units Not Meshing," *Washington Times*, April 28, 2010.

Economist. "Lawless Roads: Mexico's Southern Border," September 26, 2009.

Ellison, Jesse. "The Battle of the Anti-Violence Gurus," *Newsweek*, January 6, 2010.

Gold, Scott. "The 'Hood as a Tourist Attraction," *Los Angeles Times*, December 5, 2009.

Gray, Madison. "Experts: Street Crime Too Often Blamed on Gangs," *Time*, September 2, 2009.

Greene, Judith, and Kevin Pranis. "Gang Wars: The Failure of Enforcement Tactics and the Need for Effective Public Safety Strategies," Justice Policy Institute, July 2007. www.justicestrategies.org/files/Gang_Wars_Full_Report_2007.pdf.

Howe, Darcus. "Our Youngsters Don't Need These Saviours," *New Statesman*, May 19, 1998.

Keilthy, Paul. "They Have Names Like Massive and Posse but How Serious Is the Gang Threat on Our Streets?," *Camden New Journal* (London), October 4, 2007.

Kennedy, David. "Making Communities Safer: Youth Violence and Gang Interventions that Work," Testimony before House Judiciary Subcommittee on Crime, Terrorism, and Homeland Security, February 15, 2007. http://judiciary.house.gov/hearings /printers/110th/33314.pdf.

Klein, Melissa. "Gang Grief: Violence Wounds Teens and Communities," *Current Health 2, A Weekly Reader Publication*, March 2009.

Knight, Meribah. "For Many Latina Teens, Gang Life Adds to Stress," *New York Times*, February 21, 2010.

Mack, Kristen. "Weis: Gangs Behind Bulk of Weekend Shootings," *Chicago Tribune*, June 21, 2010.

Marquand, Robert. "France Passes New Law to Ban 'Gangs,'" *Christian Science Monitor*, June 30, 2009.

Mason, Gary. "With Love from Prison: Guatemala's Gangs," *Globe and Mail* (Toronto, ON), January 7, 2008.

New York Times. "The Wrong Approach to Gangs," July 19, 2007.

Pappa, Lauren Todd. "Gangs: Keep Out! Three Teens Tell Why Gangs Are on the Rise and What You Can Do to Stay Safe," *Junior Scholastic*, November 26, 2007.

Paradis, Jerry. "Gangs and Drugs: It's Time to Try Something New, to Get New Results," *Canadian Dimension*, July/August 2009.

Potter, Andrew. "Jihad with a Hip-Hop Pose Is an Easier Sell with Youth," *Maclean's*, July 21, 2008.

Rhee, Foon. "The Conversation: Can Kids at Play Help Defeat Gangs?," *Sacramento Bee*, January 30, 2011.

Schiller, Dane. "Feds Chase Cartel Allies in U.S. Gangs," *Houston Chronicle*, April 5, 2010.

Schrader, Jordan. "Graffiti Grab Attention of Cities, Public," *USA Today*, May 12, 2009.

Schulte, Brigid. "In War Against Gangs, It's One Kid at a Time," *Washington Post*, March 20, 2008.

Shenoy, Rupa. "The Warriors: Hardened by Gang Life, Many Young Latinos Leaving Prison Now Are Using Their Toughness to Help Others," *Chicago Reporter*, March 2005.

Smalley, Suzanne, and Evan Thomas. "The Draw of 'Dead Town,'" *Newsweek*, February 16, 2009.

Tadina, Catherine. "Choosing the Right Path: Gangs or Success," *Colt Quarterly Online*, March 11, 2011. http://coltquarterly.word press.com.

Washington Times. "Hispanic Gang Threat Overblown, Study Says," February 8, 2007.

Wells, Mike. "Gee Disputes Report Calling Gang Threat Exaggerated," *Tampa Tribune*, July 19, 2007.

Willon, Phil. "Development of Anti-Gang Academy Moves Ahead," *Los Angeles Times*, January 8, 2010.

Wilson (NC) Daily Times. "Hard Line Has to Be Drawn on Gangs," March 20, 2009.

Wood, Daniel B. "In New Tactic, L.A. Goes After Gangs' Money," *Christian Science Monitor*, January 15, 2009.

Websites

The FBI: Federal Bureau of Investigation (www.fbi.gov). This website includes an extensive section called "Gangs" that includes links to gang-related news articles and press releases as well as numerous resources about law enforcement antigang initiatives, FBI cases, and ways for communities to stop gang activity.

Florida Department of Corrections (www.dc.state.fl.us). This website includes a section called "Gang and Security Threat Group Awareness," which offers general information about gangs in the United States as well as specific details about prison gangs, supremacy groups, and gang affiliations in Los Angeles and in Florida.

National Criminal Justice Reference Service (www.ncirs.gov). The section of this website called "In the Spotlight: Gangs" includes statistics about gang activity, links to numerous government agency publications about gangs and youth crime, and descriptions of various state and local gang-related initiatives.

Index

Picture Credits